William Angus Knight

Essays in Philosophy

Old and New

William Angus Knight

Essays in Philosophy
Old and New

ISBN/EAN: 9783337073541

Printed in Europe, USA, Canada, Australia, Japan

Cover: Foto ©ninafisch / pixelio.de

More available books at **www.hansebooks.com**

ESSAYS IN PHILOSOPHY

OLD AND NEW

BY

WILLIAM KNIGHT

PROFESSOR OF MORAL PHILOSOPHY AND POLITICAL ECONOMY
IN THE UNIVERSITY OF ST ANDREWS

BOSTON AND NEW YORK
HOUGHTON, MIFFLIN AND COMPANY
The Riverside Press, Cambridge
1890

To My Friend,

JAMES RUSSELL LOWELL,

This Volume

IS DEDICATED.

PREFACE.

Several of the essays in this volume were published in London in the year 1879. A year or two afterwards, the entire stock of the book of which they formed part was destroyed by fire in the premises of Messrs. Kegan Paul & Co. It has since been out of print. The substance of the first two essays — on " Idealism and Experience, in Literature, Art, and Life," and on " The Classification of the Sciences " — was embodied in a course of lectures delivered last summer to the Royal Institution of Great Britain. The essay on " Immortality" was read to the Ethical Society at Toynbee Hall, East London, in 1888. The majority of the papers in the former volume were addressed either to Philosophical Societies, or to University students.

A leading idea will be found running through all these studies, "old and new." The essay on " Eclecticism " explains a doctrine and a tendency which pervade the volume, and color it throughout. Only one or two of the perennial problems, however, — those questions of the ages, which reappear in all the literature of Philosophy, — are discussed ; and these are dealt with less in relation to the tendencies of the time than in their permanent aspects.

In the first essay an attempt is made to test the merits of the rival philosophies of Idealism and Experience by a study of their results, or what they have given rise to in the literary and artistic products of the world, and in character both individual and national. Both of these philosophies are recognized as containing fundamental truths, and each as balancing the other.

In the essay on "The Classification of the Sciences" I have tried to rearrange the recognized groups of knowledge from a fresh point of view.

The aim of the paper on "Metempsychosis" is to prove that the preëxistence and the immortality of the soul are twin ideas, in close speculative alliance, and to show how the former casts light upon the latter.

The third essay,—originally an inaugural address, delivered to the students of Moral Philosophy in St. Andrews—and part of the fifth, discuss the theory of Evolution. As this is the most definite philosophical idea underlying the methods and processes of Science, and as its advocates claim for it the merit, not only of accounting for the modifications of organic structure, but also of explaining the origin of our intellectual and moral nature,—and as opposition to its efficacy in the latter sphere is so much misunderstood,—one or two additional paragraphs on the subject may be inserted in this prefatory note.

I do not deny the evolution of intellectual and moral ideas. I only deny that their evolution can explain their origin. Every valid theory of derivation must start with the assumption of a derivative Source, or it performs the feat of educing something out of nothing, nay of developing everything out of nonentity. It may surely rank as an axiom that whatever is subsequently evolved must have been originally involved.

Our intellectual and moral nature bears the most evident traces of evolution. Within the historic period, the progress of humanity, both in knowledge and feeling, has been more rapid and more apparent than any advance made in the type of physical organization. If we compare the records of civilization in ancient Egypt and Assyria with that of England in the nineteenth century, the mind and character of the race seem to have undergone a relatively much greater development than its physique. It is true that this may be only *apparent.* Possibly the alteration may have been equally great in both directions. It has certainly been equally real ; although between the faces carved on the stones and gems of the centuries B. C. and those we see in the nineteenth century A. D. there is less apparent difference than exists between the science, the art, the religion, and the morals of the respective periods.

Be this as it may, the history of humanity is the story of an ever-evolving, ever-developing process. No one can rationally deny, and scarcely any one ventures to question this. No individual can escape the modifying force of hereditary influences, and if these produce change in one department of our nature, they necessarily affect the whole of it. It is therefore certain that the present intellectual and moral ideas of the race are the result of ages of gradual growth, refinement, and self-rectification. Nor can it be doubted, I think, that the process has been a development from within, while it has been modified by influences from without ; that forces *ab ex-tra* have coöperated with powers and tendencies *ab intra* in producing the result.

It may be confidently affirmed that each man is what he now is, not only in virtue of what every other man has been before him, in the direct line of ancestry, but also in virtue of what everything else has been ; while it may be as confidently affirmed that he is what he is, in virtue of what he has made himself, both as a rational being and a moral agent. Such is the solidarity of the race, and its organic unity, that the present is the outcome as well as the sequel of the past, and that all the "characteristics of the present age" are due to an evolving agency, latent within the universe *ab initio.* If this be so, the moral ideas which now sway the race are a heritage which have come down to it from the dawn of history, nay, from the very beginnings of existence. They reach it with the sanctions of an immeasurable past, superadded to the necessities of the present ; and the binding force of ethical maxims is not weakened, either by the fact that they are slow interior growths, or because their present form is due to the myriad modifications of external circumstance. In either case, and on both grounds, they have the prestige of the remotest antiquity; and even if their sole *raison d'être* were the authority of custom, that authority would be real, because based upon the everlasting order of the universe. So much must be frankly admitted. The whole pith of the controversy, however, lies behind this admission.

I have pointed out in the third essay that if the intellectual and moral nature of man is entirely due to the influence of antecedents — in other words, if the past alone and by itself can explain the present, while alteration is still going on, and change is incessant — no *product* is ever reached. We have only an

eternal *process* moving on.

Πάντα ῥεῖ, οὐδὲν μένει. There is no standard

of the true, or the beautiful, or the good ; no principles of knowledge ; no canons of taste ; no laws of morality. The principles of knowledge are empirical judgments, and nothing more ; the canons of taste are subjective likings, and nothing more ; the laws of morality are dictates of expediency, and nothing more. As the fully developed doctrine of evolution abolishes species altogether, and reduces each to a passing state of the organism, which is undergoing a modification that never ceases; so the notion of a standard of the true, or of the right, vanishes, of necessity, in a process of perpetual becoming. They are always about to be ; they never really *are*. The species and the standard may still, for convenience' sake, receive a name, but it is the name of a transient phase of being, of a wave in the sea of appearance ; *vox, et preterea nihil.* The nominal alone survives ; the real and the ideal have together vanished.

As the validity of this conclusion has

been questioned, and as it seems to me of far greater moment than is often allowed, I may unfold it a little farther.

It is absolutely inevitable that all our ethical rules must undergo modification and change. That they must develop, as they have developed, is not only certain, it is an omen of hope; one of the brightest prospects on the horizon of the future. It is not difficult to discover much in the present opinion and practice of the world — in which convention so often takes the place of nature — to make us thankful that we have the prospect of change. Evolution has assuredly much still to do, both in eradicating the blots which now disfigure the belief and the actions of mankind, and in bringing out their undeveloped good. Besides, if the moral law were to operate through all time with invariable fixity, like the law of gravitation, it would be reduced to the inferior rank of mechanical necessity, and the moral agent would sink to the position of an automaton.

As to this, however, there is no controversy. Past development and future evolution are both alike admitted. The question is not whether the adult moral judgments and sentiments of the race have been preceded by rudimentary ones, and will yet ripen into maturer and mellower ones — as the bird has come out of the egg, and the oak from the acorn. The real question at issue — which no amount of brilliant discussion on side-issues should for a moment obscure — is as to the nature of the Fountain-head, not as to the character or the course of the stream. It is as to the kind of Root, out of which the tree of our knowledge has grown ; and as to the substance of the Rock, out of which our moral ideal has been hewn. Now, I maintain that evolution, pure and simple, is *process* pure and simple, with no *product ;* with nothing definitely emerging, and with nothing real or essential underneath. It is simply the Heraclitic flux of things. But this takes for granted a phenomenal theory of the universe. If noumena exist, if there be a substantial world within the ego, — or within the cosmos beyond the ego, — a doctrine of phenomenal evolution is neither the first nor the last word of Philosophy, but only a secondary and intermediate one. The whole process of development is carried on in a region entirely outside of the sphere of the philosophical problem. This problem re-emerges in full force, after every link of the chain of evolution has been traced ; and the completest enumeration of details, as to the method of development, carries us very little farther than the common-place conclusion that we, and all things else, have *grown.*

It will be found that, however far our historical inquiry into the prior phases of consciousness may be carried, it leads back to the metaphysical problem of the relation of appearances to essence, or the phenomenal to the substantial. It is only the phenomenal that can be evolved ; noumena are evolving powers or essences, themselves unevolved. If, therefore, our personality contains aught within it that is noumenal, it contains something that has not been evolved. If free will is not wholly phenomenal, — though it may have phenomenal aspects, — the will has not been developed out of desire, as desire may have been educed from sensation.

It is no solution of the difficulty, but a mere cutting of the knot, to say that will is a phase of desire, or the progeny of desire. Of course, if there be no such thing as free will, if necessitarianism be true, it is the easiest thing in the world to explain its evolution ; as easy as to explain how the flower issues from the seed, *i. e.*, it requires no explanation at all. In other words, if the rise of self-assertion be the rise of will, if to find a centre in one's self and to resist aggression or encroachment on one's rights is to discover the root of volition, the knot is cut ; but the problem is not solved. The difficulty is explained away ; but it reappears again, with undiminished force, after the explanation is given.

Everything, in this controversy, turns on the determination of the nature of personality, and its root, free will; and the whole discussion converges to a narrow issue. Unless an act be due to the personality of an agent, *i. e.*, to his antecedents, he is not only not responsible for it — it is not truly his ; similarly and *simultaneously*, unless it be due to his will, as a productive cause, it is not his, *it is the universe's ;* it is the act of the antecedent generations, and not his own act. Unless it be the outcome of his moral freedom, he is an automaton, and the act is in no sense his own.

Strong objection was taken by some critics to the statement in my essay, as originally published in *The Nineteenth Century*, that if Evolution cannot account for the origin of the moral faculty in the lifetime of the individual, the experience of

the race at large is incompetent to explain
it; because the latter is merely an extension of the same principle and the same
process. It seems to me, however, to be
self-evident that if an explanation fails in
relevancy, within a limited area filled with
phenomena of a certain class, its application to a larger area filled with the same
kind of phenomena will not redeem its
character, and give it success. If individual experience cannot explain the origin
of our moral ideas, collective experience
cannot come to the rescue; and why? Because by a mere enlargement of the space
which the principle traverses, you get no
fresh light as to its nature, or its relevancy.
It is said that the acts of all our ancestors
have transmitted a habit to posterity, and
that while the iron hand of the past is
holding us, we imagine — by the trick
which custom plays unconsciously — that
certain things are innate which have been
really acquired for us by the usage of our
ancestors. This is only possible, however,

on the pre-supposition that the course of development is at once rigidly necessitarian and purely phenomenal.

But if, in individual life and experience, the rise of the higher elements out of the lower cannot be explained by the mere pre-existence of the lower, what possible right can we have to affirm that an extension of the process of evolution indefinitely far back will bring us within sight of the solution? We must have definite and verifiable evidence of the power of evolution, to explain the processes of change within the sphere of subjective experience, before we are entitled to extend it, as the sole principle explanatory of the changes that occur beyond the range of experience. Unless evolution can explain itself, we must get behind the evolving chain to find the source of its evolution. If change cannot explain change, we must go beyond what occurs to discover the cause of its occurrence; and we cannot validly take a " leap in the dark," if we have no previous experience of walking in that particular way in the light.

It will thus be seen that the problem of evolution leads back, by no intricate pathway, to the metaphysical problem of causation. If causation is simply occurrence, or mere phenomenal sequence, — as Hume and the Comtists teach, — then, evolution is the process by which all things have come to be what they are ; and the laws of evolution are the laws of phenomenal occurrence, which illustrate " the process of becoming." If this, however, is an unsatisfactory theory of causality, if causation is something more than sequence, then evolution is not the sole or the chief principle explanatory of existence, because it leaves out of account the major truth of causation itself.

The simple observation (for surely it is no discovery) that a consequent follows in the wake of an antecedent will not explain how the sequence has been accomplished ; and no extension of the time, or widening of the area, will help to explain it, because such extension and widening are simply the addition of a number of similar links to those which already constitute the chain of derivation. We get no principle explanatory of the whole, unless we find out how the first link of the chain was forged, and what it hangs on ; or, if there be no first link, and therefore no connection with a Source, unless we discover the inner tie that unites the separate links, distinct from their mere succession in time.

Further, even assuming the correctness of the theory of development, to make, say, an opinion valid, or a custom expedient, the process of going back upon their rudiments — with those large drafts on space and time which the derivative philosophy indulges in — is not requisite ; because an opinion might be true, and an act might be useful, with no precedent to back them up. They might be both true and good just as they arose, and simply because they arose. As everything is, on the same

theory, in incessant change, and each
stage of the process is equally valuable,
venerable, and respectable, both opinion
and practice can dispense with the authority of precedent. Precedent itself, in short,
breaks down on the theory of evolution.
What is the use of an appeal to an antecedent, in the case of a thing the existence of
which is necessitated, but which is itself
different from all its predecessors and from
all its successors ; a thing which, apart
from precedent and example, has as good
a right to exist as any of them ; and which
is itself not only necessitated, but also
ephemeral?

I cannot, however, pursue this discussion
further without exceeding the limits of a
preface.

WILLIAM KNIGHT.

The University, St. Andrews, N. B.

August, 1890.

CONTENTS.

	PAGE
IDEALISM AND EXPERIENCE, IN LITERATURE, ART, AND LIFE	23
THE CLASSIFICATION OF THE SCIENCES	72
ETHICAL PHILOSOPHY AND EVOLUTION	109
ECLECTICISM	173
PERSONALITY AND THE INFINITE	211
IMMORTALITY	283
THE DOCTRINE OF METEMPSYCHOSIS	316

ESSAYS IN PHILOSOPHY.

IDEALISM AND EXPERIENCE, IN LITERATURE, ART, AND LIFE.

Two great streams of tendency have flowed side by side throughout the ages, in almost equal strength and volume. These streams have given rise to two rival philosophies, that of Idealism, and that of Experience. All the philosophies of the world belong to one or other of these two classes. They are either ideal or experiential. They have been a thousand times discussed, and their evidence weighed by their advocates, on purely speculative grounds. They may be appraised, however, and their merits and demerits discerned, quite as much by the results that have flowed from them, as by their intrinsic evidence. A sure test of their philosophic value is their outcome, or the influence they have exerted on the Literature, the Art, and the Character of the periods in which they have respectively flourished. It is the aim of the following pages to point out the influence of these two streams of tendency, and to exhibit their relations. A few preliminary sentences on the nature of Philosophy and on its leading types will enable us to estimate their nature and their results.

All philosophy originates in human curiosity, in the tendency to ask questions; but it is distinguished from a mere search for information, or miscellaneous knowledge, by its being an attempt to discover a principle which underlies, and which can account for, individual experience and detached occurrences, — a principle within which the latter may be embraced, and by which it may be in part explained. Under all the varied phases which philosophy has assumed, it has been an attempt to get beneath the surface show of things, and to interpret, however inadequately, a part of that mysterious text which the universe presents to our faculties for interpretation. And as such it has been a pursuit common to all men, whether they have known it, or known it not, and whether it has been described by the old Greek term φιλοσοφία, or not. It is a popular delusion that Philosophy is a pursuit which may interest a few recluse spirits, but is not a matter about which men and women in general need concern themselves, or with which they are competent to deal. The truth is that whenever we ask the meaning of anything, or the reason for anything, we at once begin to philosophize ; and we are all unconscious metaphysicians long before we read a word of philosophical literature. We cannot carry on the simplest conversation on common things without using terms which are the battlefields of metaphysical discussion ; and if we are to use them rationally (even in our common conversation), we must know something of their import, and something of their history, as well as of their latent significance ; that is to say, we must philosophize. If we try to distinguish between appearance and reality, between symbols and the things they symbolize, between the accidental and the essential, we are dealing with Philosophy. Nay, if we pursue the simplest inquiry far enough, we come to the question of its ultimate evidence, and that is again to say we come to its philosophy ; so that our only choice is, not whether we will deal with philosophical problems or not, but whether we will deal with them wisely or foolishly, whether we will think with reason or without it.

This being the aim and the end of Philosophy, it is evident that its cultivation must be a radical want of human nature, and its pursuit a perennial tendency. At particular periods it may be crushed under the influence of other tendencies that pronounce it to be illusory. But history shows that Philosophy always revives in undiminished strength and with increasing lustre after every temporary repression. Its best symbol is the phœnix, which was fabled to spring immortal from the fire that consumed it.

It is unnecessary, however, to vindicate philosophy any further. I have rather to illustrate the following thesis, viz., that the particular type of speculation which we either inherit or adopt has the closest bearing upon all our other opinions and tendencies, and to a large extent determines these ; and, further, that the whole complex outcome of a nation's life is colored by its philosophy, up to at least one half of what it becomes. No one can follow the course of history without perceiving that the labor of those who founded the great systems of opinion has told, in innumerable ways, upon the world at every point ; and that the various types of literary work, of artistic labor, of social sentiment, of political activity, and of religious belief, have all been modified by the philosophy which happened to be in the ascendant. The reason is very evident. It is due to the unity and the solidarity of the human race; in other words, to the fact that no element in civilization is or can be isolated from its allies.

But what are the two schools of philosophy which have always existed side by side, and are ineradicable features in the speculative life of the world? They are respectively the philosophies of Idealism and of Experience. They have succeeded each other by action and reaction, sometimes slowly and sometimes swiftly. They have assumed new phases at every stage of their evolution ; but they have never been absent, have never been extinguished — like the two great political parties, which have in every age (though under divers names) contended for supremacy, but the continued existence of both of which seems essential to the stability of nations, and the progress of the race. There is a risk, however, that we become entangled by our phraseology and deceived by the very terms we employ. We must therefore explain what is meant by the phrases we have used.

Suppose, then, that after the most extended and exhaustive study of the universe that surrounds us, — of all that appeals to our senses, and of the forces working around us and within, — the only thing we can say, in explanation of the ever-changing spectacle, is that certain of the phenomena which resemble each other can be arranged in classes, or departmental groups, and that the whole of the phenomena have been evolved out of antecedent conditions ; but that we are quite unable to rise above the stream of occurrences, and apprehend a principle working within it, or to get beyond the whole series, to what is substantial, underworking, and permanent, — this is the philosophy of Experience or of Empiricism. It is so called because it limits us to the things which come and go, which arise and fall, which appear and disappear, which are born and die, in endless sequence and by predetermined necessity. It affirms that those paths which *seem* to carry us beyond phenomena are tracks which lead nowhere; and that any apparent light as to the realm of substance is a will-o'-the-wisp, an *ignis fatuus*.

Suppose, on the other hand, that we are able to discern something more than mere co-existence, succession, and evolution, — a stable element within the changing series, a permanent causal Power working within the mutable world of mere appearance; and if, in consequence of this, we may validly interpret the things of sense as the types, the shadows, and the symbols of higher realities, viz., those *archetypes* which are not visible, nor audible, nor tangible, but which are disclosed to reason by the aid of sense, and which illumine the realm of sensation, — this is the philosophy of Idealism.

Each of these philosophies represents a fundamental tendency of human nature. Each has had a long and a distinguished history. They began to develop themselves in the remote East, before the Hellenic civilization crystallized and defined them sharply ; and they have flowed on ever since, in two great streams of tendency, distinct from each other, yet showing curious affinities, and even forming temporary alliances. It is worthy of a passing remark that, in almost every philosophical controversy, we find the central point of the opposite system somehow recognized by the system that controverts it ; only it is subordinated to another principle which has the place of honor. Thus the difference between opposite systems of philosophy lies very often in the amount of emphasis they throw on principles which both recognize.

Amongst the great idealists of antiquity there was an illustrious succession in Greece before the time of Plato ; but in him, and his intellectual work, Greek idealism culminated ; so much so that his name, more than that of any other in the history of the world, is associated with what is called "the ideal theory" of knowledge, and of existence.

It was out of an analysis of sense-perception that this theory took its rise. Following the lesser light of the previous idealism of Greece, and the greater light of the ideal within his own mind, Plato maintained that the senses — those original gateways of communication with the outer world — yield us by themselves only a mass of separate impressions, which do not constitute true knowledge, but are merely its raw material ; and that, in order to reduce these impressions to order, something more than sensation is required. He held that the mind brought forward from within, and impressed upon the phenomena of sense, certain ideal forms ; and that the exercise of this interior power was necessary to give permanence to the fleeting impressions of sense, and to build them into unity. It was the function of the reason to apprehend a substantial and permanent element underlying material forms, — and yet transcending them, — an element which existed apart both from the realm of matter and from the mind that realized it. Plato always spoke, however, of ideas in the plural. They were eternal and immutable essences, superior to the visible forms in which they were mirrored to us, and independent of the shadows which they cast. They were the archetypes of what appeared in the lower world of sense, in which they were casually reflected to us; but they were not the creation of the human faculties, "projections of the mind's own throwing." They were independent, eternal, archetypal essences, far more real than the phenomena of sense; and Plato thought that, by means of these ideas, he could explain the lower world of appearance.

There were many inconsistencies in Plato's idealism. That, however, is a very unimportant matter, because no philosophy has ever escaped the charge of harboring inconsistent elements within it, and it would be a very dull and uninteresting philosophy if it did! The great merit of the philosophy of Plato is the stress it threw upon the universal element underived from sense, which works through it and irradiates it. It is quite true that he disparages the sensible world unduly; and hence a reaction from his extreme idealism was inevitable. His great successor, Aristotle, broke with his master mainly on this one point. The theory that reduced our knowledge of individual objects by themselves to a knowledge of shadows seemed to Aristotle an undue disparagement of the things of sense. He believed that individual objects were more real than anything they symbolized, more real than the type or class to which they belonged ; and this fundamental difference between the two great philosophies of antiquity ripened gradually into the leading controversy of the Middle Ages, a controversy which three centuries of debate did not exhaust ; viz., whether genera and species were real things, or merely the names which we affix to a number of particular things. The philosophy which Aristotle championed tended more and more toward the side of experience, even sensational experience; although in the high prerogative which he assigned to Reason, both in his intellectual and in his moral philosophy, he is not to be confounded with the leaders of the latter schools, who have assigned to it the menial office of being a sort of lion's provider to the senses.

The reaction which took place in Greek philosophy after Plato was a descent from the ideal to the actual, a return to the concreate world of experience, to finite reality, to the limited and the particular. As contrasted with this, the great and prevailing merit of Plato's philosophy is not any particular doctrine which he taught, but that spirit of idealism in which his whole philosophy lived, and moved, and had its being. It was a philosophy of aspiration, of intellectual flight and moral soaring above realization toward the unattained and the infinite. The philosophy of Aristotle kept close to the finite, and distrusted all that transcended it. It gave no scope for aerial voyages, whether of the reason, or of the imagination, or of the fancy. It had, it is true, a sobering effect upon some of the vague and mystic tendencies which the opposite philosophy had shown, and which it has often subsequently fostered. It is also true that when we are in the company of Aristotle and the Aristotelians there is no fear of our mistaking a mirage for the solid land. But, on the other hand, since we are debarred from access to the transcendental, the wings of aspiration are bound, if they are not clipped; and with the repression of enthusiasm hope is diminished, and one great stimulus to progress removed.

So much for the main features of the philosophies of Idealism and Experience.

It is the *outcome* of these rival systems that we have now to investigate ; and their real character may be ascertained quite as much by the consequences to which they have given rise, as by a study of their intellectual structure and relations.

We have first to note the effect of the prevalence of the spirit of Idealism on Literature, and the contrary effect of the prevalence of Experientialism or Empiricism. Whenever the philosophy of idealism has been in the ascendant we invariably find a free and forward movement in imaginative Literature. Originality abounds, and new departures are made in many directions. The reason is obvious. Dissatisfaction with past attainment is inseparable from idealism. It is one of the surest symptoms of its presence that what has been already realized or achieved ceases to interest, or at least to attract, for the time ; and one of its immediate results is fresh creative effort, or new literary productiveness. It is emphatically true of it, under all its aspects, that "forgetting what is behind, it reaches out to what is before." All the higher literature, and especially all the loftiest poetry of the world, is permeated through and through by this spirit. From its early springtime in the Vedic hymns, its sublime flights in the Hebrew Psalter, its marvelous diffusion in the Greek literature of the age of Pericles, its appearance here and there in the Zendavesta, till it burst upon the world with unparalleled intensity at the commencement of the Christian era, we may trace its onward movement, coloring all the nobler productions of mediævalism and of modern Europe. The poetry of Dante, *e. g.*, is idealistic to the core. The spirit of chivalry is one of its effects. It breathes through all the hymns and litanies of Christendom, and is impressed in indelible lines on its architecture, from the stateliest minster to the humblest chapel ; and whenever there has been what is called a "renaissance," or revival, in literature or in art, it has been due to the working, and at times to the fermenting activity, of this principle. In Chaucer we find it mingling in strange ways, and giving an indefinable charm to his simple naturalism. Then to what are we to attribute the uniqueness of that cen-

tral product of our western civilization
whose appearance marks the highest point
that has been reached in the literature of
the world, — (our English Shakespeare,) —
but to the new spirit of idealism that
blended with his realism more naturally
and more completely than in any of his
predecessors; the one tendency giving him
his breadth and range, the other his depth
and height; and the two in unison giving
him unapproachable strength and uniqueness in literature. The modern German
renaissance, under Goethe and Schiller as
leaders, — but which shows a bright con-
stellation of lesser stars around these two,
— was characterized by an equally profound idealism. The literary work of these
men allied itself naturally to the philosophy
of Plato amongst the ancients, and to that
of Jacobi and Fichte amongst their contemporaries. When we recross the Channel, and examine the modern English poetry, at the commencement of this century,
we find that all the great writers, however
diverse the type of their genius, were animated by the same spirit, and developed
the same tendencies. We may take a
stanza from Shelley's poem *To the Skylark*

as the metaphorical embodiment of the whole movement : —

> Higher still, and higher
>   From the earth thou springest,
> Like a cloud of fire ;
>   The blue deep thou wingest.
> And singing still dost soar, and soaring ever singest.

If now for the sake of contrast we go back to the period of the Sophists in Greece, — those wonderfully clever talkers who preceded Socrates, and taught rhetoric to the people, — we find that these men were all experientialists. They worked with a utilitarian aim. They succeeded in developing an admirable prose style ; but there was no poetry amongst the Sophists, and there could be none. Literary effort turned toward the higher problems of human destiny would have been distasteful to them ; that which showed an aspiration after the unattained would have been unintelligible to them. But when the idealistic reaction began, under Socrates and Plato, we find a parallel development in literary art, preëminently in that of Sophocles. Similarly in the long Middle Age, when the philosophy of Aristotle was all dominant in the universities and schools of Europe, scarcely one poetic gleam irradiated the intellectual firmament ; but when the literary revival set in, it was the star of Plato that first rose above the horizon in the Florentine school, under the rule of the Medici, and the rise of Italian art and poetry was the return of idealism.

With the sixteenth century came many new lights on old problems ; and the prose literature of the Reformation is full of ideal tendencies. The sixteenth is, however, a difficult century to deal with. When we reach the eighteenth our footing is surer, and the illustrations ready to hand. The eighteenth was, in many respects, a monumental century, and it is easy to see how the dominant philosophy affected its literature. In France the philosophy of the Encyclopædists was supreme. In the last decade of the previous century, Bayle's Dictionary had been published. In the earlier part of the eighteenth came Voltaire, Condillac, Helvetius ; in the latter half, Diderot, and D'Alembert. The idealism of Descartes, of Malebranche, and the Port Royalists had again given place to a philosophy of experience. It was *Aristotle redivivus,* with the best part of

Aristotle left out. In England the philosophy of Locke, which ushered in the century, led on to that of Hume, Smith, and Hartley. The prevailing spirit was that of analysis, and logical test; everything hitherto received being dragged into the light, subjected to cross-examination, and compelled to exhibit its credentials. It was the sophistic era of modern European philosophy — the reappearance of the old doctrine of experience on a gigantic national scale. The result on the literature and the art of the period is noteworthy. Compare it with the state of matters in the seventeenth century in France, when the Cartesian idealism was still coloring the literature of that country, and producing such results as Corneille in poetry and Claude Lorraine in art. Of French poetry in the eighteenth century there was none. There was plenty of science, and a good deal of excellent political economy; but it was a prosaic era, matter-of-fact to the very core, unideal in its art, and as to all imaginative work, poverty-stricken. Voltaire is the typical child of the era and the movement. In Britain David Hume is the central representative; and the prevailing strain of

English poetry from Addison onwards — through Pope, Young, Dyer, Akenside, Collins, etc. — is utterly unideal. Of course there were compensations. There was a notable development of literary criticism, many brilliant essays, histories, and novels ; but just as the Greek Sophists, in a period of disintegration and analysis, contributed nothing toward the re-statement or re-interpretation of the perennial problems, acquiescing in phenomena, bowing before the omnipotence of events, with no gleam of aspiration, no touch of enthusiasm — but most diligent collectors of facts, careful students of the real, and attaining to great perfection in the writing of clever prose — such were the eighteenth century Encyclopædists in France and in England. This concentration upon facts limited the significance and the value of the contributions which they made to literature.

The two tendencies — the idealistic and the realistic — have a notable illustration in the way in which the histories of nations have been written. We have empirical historians and ideal historians. We have historians who are merely analysts or recorders, the chroniclers of events ; and

we have historians who are interpreters,
who tell us what events signify, who divine
their causes, and appraise their inner
meaning, as well as narrate their outcome
or their issues. It may be thought that
what we mainly need in a book of history
is an accurate chronicle, and that what
posterity will chiefly require is literal detail, rigid matter-of-factness. In the first
place, however, the dry record of fact
never satisfies the student of history. Lifeless statistics are as dull reading as lists
of dates, or words in a dictionary. In the
second place, we do not escape inaccuracy,
or get any nearer to reality, by the help of
histories written after that fashion. The
historian has to deal not with automata,
but with the living characters of a bygone
age ; and, as he brings his pieces on the
chess-board of his chronicle, he must show
them to us living, moving, and struggling,
as they once did in the flesh, and not present us with a mere lifeless epitome of
their deeds. The idealist is in a better
position for writing a faithful history than
the experientialist is, because he is more
likely to take account of the interior
springs of conduct, and the multitudinous

hidden forces that sway human action. Similarly, we have realist and idealist biographies; the former giving only the dry bones of fact, a skeleton of events, the latter giving an interpretation of them.

Turning now to the outcome of the two tendencies (the ideal and the real) in Art, the illustrations are even more evident. Art, in all its sections, deals with the beautiful; but, to the philosophy, or the doctrine — for it cannot be called a philosophy except by courtesy — which traces everything back to sensation, the beautiful is simply that which pleases us. It has no intrinsic place or significance in objects beyond us. According to this doctrine there is nothing essentially beautiful, or inherently admirable, in the universe. The difference — which is an all important one to the opposite philosophy — between what happens to be agreeable and what is in itself beautiful is ignored. All standards are relative or accidental. Empiricism in Art virtually says they are all good enough in their way, because they have happened to emerge, but there is nothing inherent in any one of them. Idealism in Art affirms, on the contrary, that there is but one absolute standard of the beautiful, which all workers in Art endeavor to reach, and realize in various ways, but to which no one ever fully attains.

If we now examine the effect of the two tendencies on the history of Art, and on the course of its development, we find that the effect of empiricism on the French art of the eighteenth century was precisely similar to its influence on literature. In that dull century there was no art worthy of the name. It was the era and the period of the *illumination*, as it was presumptuously called, — because there was really no light on ultimate questions, — unless the term was adopted on the satirical principle of *lucus a non lucendo.* When the Encyclopædists were the dictators of Europe in mental science and in literature, all knowledge being traced back to sensation and represented as its outgrowth, Art became of necessity mechanical and prosaic. It grew formal and technical, rigid in its conformity to rule and precedent, devoid of originality, deficient even in freedom. What a descent from the strong men, who, breathing the air of the Cartesian idealism, had glorified the French art of the seventeenth century. The eighteenth is, of all modern eras, the one in which empiricism in Art most distinctively flourished. The period in which idealism flourished most was from the fourteenth to the sixteenth century, especially in the great Tuscan school of Italy. Contemporaneously with its outburst in the poetry of Dante was its early embodiment in the art of Giotto, and Niccola Pisano, and such of their successors as Donatello, Fra Angelico, Lucca de la Robbia, Filippo Lippi, Girlandaio, till we come down to Bellini, in whom the two tendencies — the natural and the ideal — were united. In Giovanni Bellini we find the most consummate perfection of execution combined with rare ideal features; but when we pass Bellini and the almost equally noticeable Botticelli and Carpaccio, and — omitting Raphael — come down to Titian and Tintoretto, we find that the mere power of technical mastery in dealing with subjects (*i. e.*, the literal and the actual) interfered with the ideal, and almost brushed it aside. It pushed out the imaginative expression of art ; and the result was that, with all their perfection of form, and gorgeousness of color, there was a certain coarseness in these later Venetian masters. We miss the nobler reserve and refinement of their predecessors.

Mr. Ruskin has written much, and to profit, on this subject throughout his works ; but he has said nothing better, and nothing so clear, as Browning has done in several of his lyrics, most notably in the poem called *Old Pictures in Florence*. The theme of this poem is the contrast between Greek art and the art of Christendom. After a fine exordium, the comparison is drawn.

> May I take upon me to instruct you ?
> When Greek Art ran and reached the goal,
>   Thus much had the world to boast *in fructu* —
> The Truth of Man, as by God first spoken,
>   Which the actual generations garble
> Was re-uttered.

Then he gives the effect of this Greek art.

> So, you saw yourself as you wished you were,
>   As you might have been, as you cannot be ;
> Earth here, rebuked by Olympus there :
>   And grew content in your poor degree,
> With your little power, by those statues' godhead,
>   And your little scope, by their eyes' full sway,
> And your little grace, by their grace embodied,
>   And your little date, by their forms that stay.

So, testing your weakness by their strength,
  Your meagre charms by their rounded beauty,
Measured by Art in your breadth and length,
  You learned — to submit is a mortal's duty.

And now note, in contrast to this sub-mission before the omnipotence of realized fact, — which was the outcome or final lesson of Greek art, — the counter truth and the counter tendency.

Growth came when, looking your last on them all,
  You turned your eyes inwardly one fine day,
And cried with a start — What if we so small
  Be greater and grander the while than they?
Are they perfect of lineament, perfect of stature?
  In both, of such lower types are we
Precisely because of our wider nature;
  For time, theirs — ours, for eternity.

To-day's brief passion limits their range,
  It seethes with the morrow for us and more.
They are perfect — how else? they shall never change:
  We are faulty — why not? we have time in store.
The Artificer's hand is not arrested
  With us; we are rough-hewn, no-wise polished:
They stand for our copy, and, once invested
  With all they can teach, we shall see them abolished.
. . . .

It was under the inspiration of this idea that, according to Browning, the early Florentine painters worked; feeling that they themselves and their contemporaries, with their present aims and coming des-

tiny, were more worthy of representation
by art than any of the old forms of the
Greek divinities, which expressed but the
fleeting fashion of their day ; and so
Browning continues : —

On which I conclude, that the early painters,
  To cries of " Greek Art and what more wish you ? "—
Replied, " To become new self-acquainters,
  And paint man, man, whatever the issue !
Make new hopes shine through the flesh they fray,
  New fears aggrandize the rags and tatters :
To bring the invisible full into play !
  Let the visible go to the dogs — what matters ? "

Give these, I exhort you, their guerdon and glory
  For daring so much, before they well did it.
The first of the new, in our race's story
  Beats the last of the old ; 't is no idle quiddit.

Perhaps in all literature there is no
better or juster explanation of the difference between Greek art and the art
of Christendom ; the preëminence of the
former consisting in its finished though
limited perfection — its aim to find within
the finite the end or goal of endeavor ;
and the higher merit, the preëminence of
the latter, consisting in its dissatisfaction
with the most perfect expression of the
finite, and its effort to rise thence toward
the Infinite.

There is more, however, to be said on the contrast between these two tendencies in Art — between Literality, with imitation as its end and aim, and Ideality, with suggestion as its end and aim.

Empiricism is, of course, always magnifying *experience*, at the expense of other tendencies. Well! let us go to experience, that we may test empiricism in Art. In entering any of the modern galleries, it does not require one to have mastered Plato's Philosophy of the Beautiful to be able to tell at once what pictures are inspired by idealism, and what are not, whether they be landscape or figure paintings. In landscape, the most perfect picture is not one which is a mere imitation of nature, a semi-photographic reproduction of it. It is rather one which gives us a divination of its meaning, a disclosure of its latent soul. Such pictures as those of Turner — by far the greatest landscape artist that ever lived — pictures in which Nature is glorified by the "light that never was on sea or land," these are the outcome of idealism, or idealistic vision in Art. Similarly in portraiture the most perfect triumph is not an exact reproduction of

the outward appearance of the human face
or figure. It is not even a transcript of
one particular mood, but it is the blending
of many different moods into a likeness,
in which *expression* is all dominant, and
which combines in a unity what the person thus represented has formerly revealed
on many different occasions, and which is
therefore a truer interpretation of character behind the mask of physiognomy than
the most perfect photograph could be.

Suppose that we had, in any art gallery,
such a transcript of reality that, as in the
Greek story, the very birds of the air were
deceived, and came to pick the fruit from
the canvas, or a painted curtain was mistaken for a real one, would it satisfy any
one as a high triumph of Art? It might
satisfy a photographer, but it would not
even please a trained artistic eye. One
who has found out the secret of the beautiful wishes no such deceptive mimicry.
If Art were the mere imitation of Nature,
many would discard it, and prefer the
thing it imitated, viz., Nature itself. The
truth is that the best art always leads
from Nature to a Reality beyond it, and
the ideal artist tries to embody on canvas

what has never been disclosed to the sense of sight.

" Imitate Nature," say the Realists ; " reproduce what is before your eyes, and you can't go wrong."   Now, even if this were the true artistic rule, — which it is not, — the question would remain, What is Nature ? and that is a point by no means so easily determined as may appear upon the surface.   There are as many different and conflicting theories of Nature as there are of Life.   If Nature be not dead inanimate substance, but a living force beneath material forms, a creative source of energy endlessly changing, and everlastingly renewing itself, the reproduction or representation of this by Art will be something very different from the photograph of a single passing phase which it may have chanced to assume.   Here it is that we discern the power and the perennial charm of the landscape art of Turner.   He never reproduced a single passing phase of Nature ; but, by that marvelous second-sight of his, by the " power of a peculiar eye," he blended into one many separate and fugitive impressions, and brought them to a luminous focus.   He fused them together, not artificially but naturally, so that the result was no fanciful invention, — which would have been a travesty of Nature, — but a divination of her inmost spirit, disclosed to him through a multitude of her forms. "Turner took liberties with Nature," say some of his realistic critics, who have no inward eye like his. He did nothing of the kind. He only took this liberty with each passing mood of Nature, that he thrust it aside, if it interfered with others which were quite as real and worthy of representation; and he combined the many in the one, as no painter had ever done before him, making the fugitive permanent by the idealization of his art. Every one knows that the face of Nature is often commonplace. Dull skies, or hard gray weather, a monotony of cloud, or continual mist; these things no artist would select for reproduction on canvas. But the idealist does not merely select the more beautiful forms, and combine them into a fresh product. He goes beneath them all. While Nature is forever changing, is in incessant ebb and flow, he divines its underlying essence; and, knowing by intuition how the spirit of the beautiful clothes itself in the vesture of form, he does not care whether he has seen what he actually portrays literally unfolded before the eye of sense. He has seen it floating in more glorious vision before the eye of the spirit, and he knows it to be truer than any photograph — or the instantaneous reproduction of a passing mood of Nature — could possibly be.

We must also remember that in physical Nature imperfection mingles with every fragment of the beautiful that exists. Beauty is often hid behind the ugly, and within the commonplace ; and Art pursues the beauty, marred and mutilated as it constantly is by deformity. As Tennyson puts it, —

> That type of perfect in the mind
> In Nature we can nowhere find.

But all Art is a sort of bridge flung across the chasm which separates the actual from the ideal, the real from the transcendent.

We have noted the relation in which the art of Christendom stands to the precedent art of Hellenism ; but it is to be observed that the latter had its ideal as well as the former, and drew all its inspiration from it. Greece was emphatically the land of the ideal, and the Hellenic civilization embodied it in a multitude of ways to the ancient world. Take Greek sculpture, for example. To what do we owe the majesty and the radiance of the gods of Greece? In part, perhaps, to the free and joyous energy of the Hellenic people; but far more to that conception of Nature which was current in the noblest period of their history; and to the idea that the outward form was, at its best, an embodiment of something higher than itself. If we had the finest sculptures of the age of Pericles before us, we could not find their secret, until we passed beyond the form to the thought underlying it, to the soul within the substance of the marble, the immaterial hinted at and expressed by the material. The art of Phidias was an appeal from sense to soul, from the outward to the inward.

The Greek artists were not copyists of the actual. Their imagination was too intense and varied in its energy, to permit of their being satisfied with any single embodiment of beauty, however perfect; and their art may be said to have been a historical protest against realism, and the mere imitation either of Nature or of man. The

copyist sees only one of the fugitive phases
of the thing he copies. Both Nature and
man, however, assume new aspects every
instant. They do not tarry to be reproduced as they are, at any given moment
of time. Thus the evanescence of each
sample of the beautiful disclosed to the
senses — and the fragmentariness of the
whole series — sends us in quest of a beauty
that is one and not manifold, that is constant and not changing. We pursue the
infinitely beautiful through all the illusions
of finite beauty, and our dissatisfaction
with each embodiment of it urges us onward in pursuit of that ideal, of which
Plato in the *Symposium* sings the praise.
Those finite and detached specimens of
beauty — which we find in Poetry, Painting, Music, and Architecture respectively,
— are at times distracting, from their very
multiplicity, their immense variety, and
still more from their changefulness. We
therefore go in search of some key which
will explain each, by unfolding its relation
to the rest, and to the unity which underlies them all. Without this key, the experience of fresh beauty might even induce
a sense of weariness; but with it, each

successive instance — which illustrates the unity in the light of the variety — has the charm of novelty. The reason is obvious. It is because the key, or the explanation of the new experience, does not come out of an old one, but from that which transcends new and old alike; while it is the conviction that the highest beauty is unrepresentable by Art, or inexpressible by means of it, that gives its chief interest to all the approximations which shadow it forth.

In connection with this we may note that Raphael — who was not so idealistic as his predecessors — tells us that "as he could not find perfect beauty in the actual, he made use of an ideal which he formed for himself;" although I would rather say which he found within himself, and which nothing appealing to the eye or to the ear could possibly disclose to him.

The mention of the ear, as another channel through which the beautiful reveals itself, leads to the consideration of Music or Musical Art.

The distinction between the ideal and the actual is quite as apparent in Music as it is in any of the sister arts; and our

modern music has opened up a new channel of approach to the ideal which is pecu-
liarly and distinctively its own. Through
this medium we can, more easily than
through any other, escape from the thraldom of sense, and enter the wonderland of
ideality. Music requires no phenomenal
medium like canvas and oils, or marble, or
stone, or wood, by which to embody its
ideal ; and hence the great musicians are
less copyists of one another than other
artists are, and therefore perhaps they get
closer to reality.

If we compare the majestic creations of
John Sebastian Bach, the Shakespearean
wealth of inspiration to which Beethoven
attained, the height to which Handel and
Mozart carry us in their oratorios and
masses, the ethereal grace of Schumann,
the majesty of Wagner, and the depth of
Brahms, with the modern Italian opera,
the same distinction which we have traced
in pictorial art will be apparent. It is
worthy of note, in passing, that while it
is to Italy that we are mainly indebted for
idealism in painting, it is to Germany that
we owe idealism in music, as well as in
philosophy. It is true that in music we

have not the same sharp lines of contrast drawn between the two schools or tendencies, such as we have in philosophy, poetry, and painting. It is also true that in many a symphony, as in many an oratorio, there is much of both tendencies. The reason perhaps is that music, being an extremely delicate and subtle medium for the expression of emotion, we have of necessity mixed effects in almost every great creation. In a sonata, as in a lyric song, we may in one part (as in one stanza) be in the highest regions of ideality ; and, in another, we may descend, if not to the materialistic level, at least to the terrestrial side of things. One has only to recall the effect produced by some oratorios (or single choruses in an oratorio), by many a mass, and many a sonata, — the sense not of freedom only, but of aspiration and flight, of escape from the dull prosaic flats of existence to a more ethereal region, — and compare it with the effect produced by common dance-music, or by such a song as "Willie brewed a peck o' maut"! I say nothing against the dance-music or the song. They have their place, their function, and their charm. It is only necessary to bring out the contrast.

The great composers have doubtless followed the scientific laws of Art in writing their most ideal pieces; but, in proportion to their originality, they have broken through the trammels of precedent. They have risen above bondage to the actual, and breathed into the otherwise dry bones of musical structure the breath of their own life. There is a story told of Beethoven that when some one said to him that a particular passage in one of his compositions was incorrect, and could not be allowed by the laws of musical composition, he replied, "Then *I* allow it; let that be its justification." Here we see the creative artist, the idealist, breaking away from the slavery of use and wont, and taking a new departure by the originality of his insight.

Speaking of his symphonies, Beethoven said, "I feel that there is an eternal and infinite to be attained. Music ushers man into the portal of an intellectual world, ready always to encompass him, but which he may never encompass." In this sentence we see Beethoven's recognition of the vastness of the Ideal encircling, and enveloping, and pressing upon him contin-

ually. It suggests the lines in the *Ranolf
and Amohia* of Alfred Domett, referring
to Browning's *Sordello,* —

The vast ideal's glare,
Blasting the real, to its own dumb despair.

No one who has any music in his own
soul can fail to be aware of the fact that
there are some composers who not only
open for us a door, as it were, into the
"house called beautiful," but who compel
us to go in with them ; and who, when we
have entered, discourse to us in such a
way that the sense both of discord and illusion vanishes for the time, in the revelation of a transcendent harmony ; who help
us to escape from the glamour of mere
appearance, the wearisome reiterations of
the actual, and who take us closer to existence, to the "last clear elements of things,"
than when we are in familiar contact with
the phenomena of sense. Listen to the
Waldstein sonata, or to Beethoven's symphony in C minor, or to the second of his
sonatas dedicated to Hadyn, and you feel
that a power is at work, carrying you out
of the realm of sensation into that of
thought, — to a Rock that is higher than
you, — and disclosing your relations to the

Infinite. You find your nature expanded, and your consciousness, at one and the same time, freed and deepened. Similarly, there are other composers who keep us enchained to the actual, and never allow us to outsoar it, in any idealization of the real. The former class are all inspired — whether they know it, or are ignorant of it — by the spirit of Plato; the latter are — consciously, or unconsciously — the disciples of Aristotle.

There are nearly as many different schools of music as there are of poetry; the two extremes being, on the one side, the surface brilliancy which we have in the larger part of the Italian opera, and on the other the "great German ocean" (as it has been aptly called) of the symphony and the sonata, of the mass and the oratorio, — in which we have height and depth combined, strength, pathos, tenderness, and endless suggestiveness.

We now come to the influence of the two rival tendencies on individual and national character. In this connection I must note not only the bearing of the opposite philosophies *on* the individual, but also the conception *of* the individual to which they respectively give rise. According to the one, every human being has a separate value, an individual worth ; and with each endless possibilities are upbound. According to the other, each is like a wave of the sea, which arises on the surface and falls again ; that is to say, he is an accidental element in existence, fraught with no special significance, and destined to none. The social and political outcome of this doctrine will be apparent. A utilitarian doctrine of morals is almost invariably associated with a sensational theory of the origin of knowledge. If all our knowledge comes from sense, and may on the last analysis be traced back to it, then all our actions must spring from motives of self-interest and aggrandizement. On this theory, the rules of action which happen to sway the individual have no sanction higher than experience, inherited through ages and generations. Universal custom, or the developed tendencies of the race, constitute his rule of action.

The idealist does not underrate the force or the significance of such a rule. It has a most venerable ancestry, and indisputable secular authority. As it brings with it the prestige of all past experience, its claim to be listened to is great. But then the opposite philosophy of idealism leads the individual to recognize a law of conduct, at once "in him, yet not of him," to find himself under no mere custom, which has happened to emerge in the struggle for existence, but an absolute rule of right, which has been evolved within the race, but is superior to it, and is therefore not derived from it.

Here, as formerly, our concern is not with the evidence on which these rival philosophies of ethics repose, or by which they have been respectively championed. It is with the outcome or effect of each respectively on character. The prevalence of the one or the other of them at a particular time has been largely due to temperamental causes, and there are many advantages and many disadvantages associated with each. These ought to be impartially recognized. The effect of idealism is unquestionably to elevate the character that is pervaded by it. Sometimes, it is true, its presence makes one visionary, or quixotic. It has been even known to make its votary indifferent to that side of life which connects us with the world as it is. The unsatisfactory side of every-day experience pressing forcibly upon him, he takes refuge in Utopias, in order that he may escape from the illusions of the actual. Consequently the idealist often misses much of the satisfaction which he might derive — and which others derive — from the world as it is.

On the other hand, no dispassionate student of history, and of historical biography, can fail to see that whenever the empirical philosophy has been in the ascendant, the character of the nation, or of the period, has become prosaic and commonplace. It may have been extremely shrewd, in the midst of its commonplace — all the more shrewd, vivacious, and sparkling, perhaps, from the absence of ideality (as in the period of the French enlightenment in the eighteenth century); but as it gradually sinks to the matter-of-fact level, it at the same time degenerates to the commonplace.

The two tendencies may be compared as follows. We have, on the one hand, contentedness with the actual, acquiescence in its limits, an abject deference to facts, without any attempt to rise above them. We have, on the other hand, a certain amount of restlessness, but with the restlessness, aspiration ; an effort to surmount hindrance, and to rise, on what have well been named " the stepping-stones of our dead selves," to higher things. The effect of the pursuit of ideals on personal character is unquestionably great. These ideals are often cast down by experience, but they are not therefore destroyed. Although many of them can never be wrought out or realized, and many of them are destined to change, — it does not follow that any one of them has been useless. The very destiny of each ideal that is cherished is to give place to another, still loftier ; and this is accomplished without jealousy, and without regret. A life contented with this, which pursues the even tenor of its way with no ideality or aspiration, is apt to be at once jealous of rivals, and suspicious of change. By the pursuit of his ideals, however, and by exchanging one for another successively, the idealist gets nearer to reality than the experientialist does, by keeping to the prosaic facts which obtrude upon the senses. He has a wider range of vision, a more comprehensive outlook; and his very dissatisfaction with the actual becomes to him the happiest augury that he can outstep his past attainments, and transcend his former experience. In comparing the characters of the representative men who respectively illustrate these two streams of tendency, one may see the self-complacency and satisfaction of the experientialist, his contentedness with facts and laws. On the other hand, the dissatisfaction of the idealist, his sense of the poverty of experience, is apparent; but associated with this there is a stimulus to fresh endeavor, which lifts him out of the ruts of commonplace, and gives him wing.

How the two tendencies operate respectively on society at large is also instructive. When even the experience philosophy is in the ascendant, the liberty of the individual is more or less imperiled. One of the corollaries of that philosophy being that "might is right," the freedom of the units in the body corporate is lessened, when it gains the ascendancy. If individuals and races are regarded merely as waves that rise out of the sea of existence, and fall back to it again, the natural conclusion will be that the units composing the mass may be utilized for the common weal. They may be regarded, for example, as good fighting material, good for forming battalions, and may be dealt with accordingly in the rough, should any one arise with force of character requisite to seize and sway them for an ulterior end. In fact, the Rob Roy rule of action, —

> That they should take who have the power
> And they should keep who can, —

is the direct outcome of the one doctrine ; while a regard for the rights of the individual — and especially of the weak and the defenseless — is upbound with the other. Tyranny may not be always practiced when the former philosophy is dominant, but it is always possible. It may be the despotism of one (as in an oligarchy), or it may be the hydra-headed despotism of the many (as in some republics) ; but in either case, and in any case, the natural outcome of the philosophy, if it stands alone, is a style of action that disposes of the individual too easily. So much is this the case that any well-instructed person could infer, from the character of the prevailing philosophy, what social and political results would probably emerge in the nation or the period.

So much for the contrast of the two tendencies, and their outcome in Literature, Art, and Life. It is to be noted, however, that as tendencies of human nature, they are permanent and ineradicable. One of the two may work itself out, in the course of a generation, and then cease to be as prominent or influential as it was; but it only retires to assume new features, and to achieve new triumphs when it reappears. The doctrine of the transmutation of force, and the permanence of energy may here be applied without any abatement or scruple.

It is also to be observed that each of the two tendencies is essential to the other. Though often opposed, often in violent hostility, they are *inseparable*, and necessary each to each. It follows that neither of them can ever be all dominant in the world, so as to exclude or extinguish the other, as their partisans desire. This is just as obvious as is the distinction between them. The absolute supremacy of either is a Utopian dream. Humanity has never left itself, so to speak, without a witness of the presence of both ; and although the speech of one of them has been sometimes like " a voice crying in the wilderness " of misunderstanding or reproach, in the next generation it has received the hosannas of the multitude.

A sensational theory of the origin of knowledge, a utilitarian doctrine of morals, a conventional standard of the beautiful, a theory of society which disposes of the individual as a mere unit in the mass, all these have their use to the idealist in reminding him of his connection with mother earth, in preventing him from becoming a mere visionary, and pursuing quixotic enterprises and impracticable schemes. But, on the other hand, to the disciple of experience, who is continually reminding himself and others of his relation to the things of sense, the opposite philosophy is indispensable ; that is to say, if he is to escape, not only from the partisanship of a sect, but from the thraldom of a theory. It not only opens up to him novel points of view, in endless series, and indefinite suggestiveness ; but it supplies him with fresh inspiration and stimulus, and with a moral tonic of the greatest value. It counteracts the tendency to succumb before the apparent drift of circumstances, and to fall into that *nil admirari* mood, which is so fatal to character in an age of cynicism.

It is true that we are all born either Platonists or Aristotelians, that is to say, either idealists or empiricists; and the bias toward one or the other works on in the blood of the race, and is ineradicable by culture, or by any other influence. It would be the reverse of an advantage if the elimination of either were possible. If it would be the dullest and most disagreeable world to live in if we all agreed with each other on every conceivable point, it would be the most monotonous world imaginable if our sympathies ran always on parallel lines, and the most unprogressive world if our tendencies all met at a common focus. The great desideratum is the frank admission by every one of the value of other lines of thought and sympathy and action, while he pursues his own; the recognition, not only of their importance to those who follow them, but of their use to the world at large; so that — whether we were born Platonists or Aristotelians, whether we are now idealists or experientialists — we may attain to the catholicity and the tolerance that "shun the falsehood of extremes."

THE CLASSIFICATION OF THE SCIENCES.

It is more important to ascertain the true Principles of Classification than actually to classify the Sciences, for two reasons : first, because the schemes which exist are so numerous, almost every philosopher of note having tried to solve the problem ; secondly, because each attempt, being a product of the state of knowledge existing at the time, must share in the imperfection, as well as reflect the light of the period.

It has been said that it is of slight consequence how we arrange our knowledge, provided we do actually know what we think we know ; and further, that we should rest contented with the isolated fragments we can gather together, if we are careful to sift and to verify them. It is obvious, however, that we cannot know any one thing accurately until we know it in its relation to others ; and also unless our knowledge converges to a focus, and becomes symmetrical. The relations and co-relations of the several sciences compel us to bring them together, while we group or arrange them in some sort of order; and there is no science which does not either overlap, or intersect, or borrow from another. Each has its frontier, or intellectual margin, which is the property of several; and territorial disputes as to this common ground are frequent. While the provinces of many are not as yet accurately defined, the circle of the whole is continually widening. They have thus the very subtlest inter-relations.

The problem before us is how to arrange the sections of knowledge so that they fall into departmental groups, each of which is affiliated to its neighbor by a natural, and not by an artificial tie — in other words, by some organic principle. In addition to this, the whole series should be so arranged that if we were to start from any one of its remotest subsections, we should be able to work our way back with ease from class to class, under the guidance of a principle which at once comprehends the whole and unites the parts.

It might be thought that, in order to succeed in this, one must be acquainted with the details of all the sciences. This, of course, is absolutely impossible ; but the root principle of each science may be understood by those who know very little beyond it. The generic idea involved in a particular body of knowledge may be clearly grasped, while only a few of the details which illustrate it are known ; and it does not follow that a minute and careful study of detail would make the fundamental notion of any science clearer to the mind. In some respects the specialist who has mastered a whole realm of knowledge — perhaps created it — is less fitted than other men to determine its place in the hierarchy of the sciences. In proportion to the originality and value of his discoveries is the likelihood that he will exaggerate their importance. As a matter of fact, it is not by our most distinguished specialists that the best classifications of knowledge have been made. Looking upon their own province as paramount, they have sometimes adopted an arbitrary arrangement of the rest, as if they were satellites revolving around a central sun.

It is rather by those who have the catholicity which even a slight acquaintance with many sciences gives that the best classifications have been made.

Moreover, not only is a specialist likely to begin the work of classification with a bias, but he cannot define his own province until he transcends it. No science can be allowed to settle its own boundaries, as no nation could be safely trusted to determine its own frontier. The provinces on the map of human knowledge must be arranged by mutual adjustment and debate, at times by conflict and the arbitrament of war. The intellectual world, for example, would not allow a logician to fix the province of Logic, if he was no more than a logician ; or a Biologist to say how much his province should include, if he knew nothing beyond it.

The sciences themselves are constantly changing. Some are enlarging, others contracting and disappearing. In their mutual relations they are never stationary for an instant of time, because every discovery leads on to another, if it does not involve it ; and, if the existing bodies of knowledge are always changing, a rear-

rangement of the whole, sooner or later,
becomes inevitable. Some sciences, once
honored, are now like wrought-out mines
— an exhausted intellectual field. A district, supposed for centuries to be an independent territory, is afterwards regarded
as a subordinate province — belonging naturally, and of right, to another science.

It is obvious that no classification can
be final, simply because we cannot anticipate the future ; but the greater provinces
on the map of knowledge have been little
altered since that map was first constructed by the genius of Aristotle. They
have been like the four great Continents,
which are marked off from one another by
characteristic physical features, and their
populations distinguished by broad racial
differences. These do not alter. The
smaller districts, on the other hand — in
which the differences are merely local or
tribal — are always changing.

There are, however, no provinces in
Nature which exactly correspond with the
diagrams we construct. These diagrams
are merely our reading of the text which
Nature presents to the human faculties
for interpretation, — a subjective render-

ing of objective fact. Just as with our psychological schemes, there are no divisions in human nature itself. What we call "perception," "memory," "imagination," "reason," etc., are not compartments of mind, but the varying activities of a single principle, the unity of which is implied in the very variety of its powers. Similarly, our arrangements of the sciences are all artificial, in the sense that they are the interpretation we put upon that which exists, either within us or beyond us. It must further be remembered that, as every object in Nature affords material for several of the sciences, and can be dealt with so as to yield the conclusions of several, there must of necessity be not only an overlapping of the provinces of knowledge, but also a blending of its problems in experience.

That many artificial and arbitrary schemes of classification have been offered is not to be wondered at. *A priori* theorists have tried to arrange a programme of all possible knowledge — drawing out a chart which would remodel Nature. They have presumed to tell us how the sciences *ought to* develop themselves, or how they should have arisen historically. The sciences have not arisen, however, in the order of logical sequence, or of their theoretic distinction from one another. They have sprung up in the most heterogeneous manner, and have been developed in the most casual fashion, as province after province has been explored. A chart of the sciences, constructed according to the time of their historical appearance, would be interesting and extremely useful; more especially if at the same time it traced out the often complex causes that have given rise to them. Were such a chart drawn out, however, it would be found to be totally unlike the philosophical classification of which we are in search. The order of time and the order of nature are very different.

An opposite opinion was advanced by Comte. He affirmed that the organic or structural arrangement of knowledge followed the line of its historical evolution. If this were the case, our chief if not our sole guide to the classification of the sciences would be the history of the human mind, and of its efforts to understand the universe. The theory of Comte is untrue to fact. Looking to the history of the rise of the sciences, we find that the movements have not been always linear, so to speak; the most progressive ones have been sometimes circular. Sciences last in the order of nature have been first in the order of time; and, what is equally noteworthy, many causes — intellectual, social, and political combined — have determined their origin. Some have sprung out of the dark, as it were, into light, at particular times, and in unexpected places. Contrariwise, when one would expect a discovery to have been made, — because it followed logically from a truth already known, — it was not made. The door remained shut in that direction, and a considerable time elapsed before it was opened.

In the further discussion of this question much will depend upon the definitions with which we start; and almost everything turns on the meaning we attach to Science itself. As the term is sometimes used with the utmost vagueness, — and the result is mere confusion, — we must distinguish Science, on the one hand, from the inferior knowledge which it supersedes; and, on the other hand, from the higher knowledge which transcends it. We must separate the Sciences, both from miscellaneous information and from Philosophy, as well as from Art. Some people talk of the "philosophical sciences"—a phrase that is quite as misleading as its opposite, the "scientific philosophies." Others speak of the "practical sciences"—a phrase just as satisfactory as it would be to talk of "scientific practice." It is true that these phrases are not misleading if they are taken figuratively, and if we keep in mind that we are making use of symbols. At the same time it is absolutely necessary to remember that knowledge is wider than science, and includes much more than science within it. Scientific knowledge is a knowledge of phenomena, or groups of phenomena, belonging to provinces marked off from one another by distinct intellectual boundaries, and all reduced to law; and our knowledge becomes scientific as soon as we find out the law of the occurrence of phenomena, so as to explain their recurrence.

What follows from this is significant. It is outside the province of science to investigate the nature of substance. That is the province of Philosophy; and when we raise the question of the ultimate essence of all things, it is a problem of philosophical theology. Theology is not a science. If theology were a science, God would be a phenomenon. There is a science of Religion, because the phenomena of the human mind, in its effort to apprehend that which lies beyond Nature, can be classified, and so far explained; but there can be no science of the Infinite. It is true that we might scientifically explain the results of any manifestation of the Infinite, in Nature or in History; and therefore, to that extent, we might have a science of theology; but we cannot place it within the circle of those sciences which have for their object-matter the phenomena of the universe.

The distinction between Philosophy and Science is ultimate and radical. The aim of Science is the increase of knowledge, by the discovery of laws, within which all phenomena may be embraced, and by means of which they may be explained. The aim of Philosophy, on the other hand, is *to explain the sciences*, by at once including and transcending them. It does not,

on the one hand, merely prepare the way
for science ; nor, on the other, is its function a simply administrative one ; viz., to
arrange the provinces of knowledge. Its
office is to take up the problem after it
has been laid down by science, and to
carry it further. Its sphere is that of Substance and Essence. It is a search for
the *Ding-an-sich*, the *causa causans*, within
the realm of the Infinite and the Absolute,
the discovery and interpretation of which
give it a title to rank — if we may speak
in a figure — as the *scientia scientiarum*.
In so far as any science deals with this
question of substance, it is occupying itself with the problem of philosophy under
an altered name. As compared with all
scientific questions, that problem varies
not. It has been the quest of the ages to
apprehend the Reality that underlies appearance, to unfold its characteristics, and
to explain its relation to the phenomenal
world, in which it is shadowed forth by
type and symbol.

While this remains, through all the
changes of the schools, the perennial question of Philosophy, it is approached from
so many sides, and in such different ways,

that a variable element is introduced along-side of the permanent one. This may explain why no philosophical theory lasts, why all are superannuated soon after they take shape in propositions or formulæ, though each reappears again in slightly altered form.

The attempts made to classify the sciences may be counted, not by the score, but by the hundred and the thousand. Almost every philosopher has tried to solve the problem.

In ancient times the classifications of Plato and of Aristotle were the most memorable. Aristotle — whose philosophy was of the most encyclopædic character — surveyed the entire domain of human knowledge, and himself created several sciences by his extraordinary architectonic faculty. He wrote — or dictated — books on Logic, on Metaphysics, on Morals, on Politics, on Rhetoric, on Natural History, on Zoölogy and Comparative Anatomy, on Physics and Astronomy, on the art of Poetry, and on Psychology. All this was with him a classification of Philosophy rather than of Science. He divided Philosophy into the theoretical, the productive, and the prac-

tical domain : the theoretical embracing
physics, mathematics, and metaphysics ;
the productive including the various arts ;
while the practical included ethics and politics.   Aristotle's classification, however,
has many defects.   Logic, for example, is
outside of it — although he was the first
to formulate the laws of deductive reasoning in a systematic manner ; and the distinction between productive and practical
science is a very misleading one.   Why
should politics be regarded as a practical,
and not as a productive science ?   If we
take into account the end it seeks to accomplish, it is more productive than the
sciences included by Aristotle under the
latter head.   It is a mistake, however, to
classify knowledge with any reference to
its aims.   Its inherent nature must be the
basis of any successful classification ; and
it must be confessed that, while Aristotle
arranges the sciences for us after a fashion,
— and in a very remarkable way, — he
neither shows us their evolution from a
central principle, nor builds them up into
an organic whole.   With all his greatness,
he fails both as a scientific architect, and
as an interpreter of the order of nature.

The first really important classification in modern times was that of Francis Bacon ; and the most famous that have followed are those of Hobbes, Comenius, Locke, Leibnitz, Vico, Kant, Fichte, Schelling, Hegel, Coleridge, Comte, Ampère, Rosmini, Whewell, Hamilton, Herbert Spencer, and Mr. Bain. Those of Bacon, Hegel, Comte, and Spencer may be briefly glanced at.

Bacon's intellect was, like Aristotle's, encyclopædic ; and he tried to map out the sciences, after first laying down a new organon or method of inquiry. He divided all knowledge into a knowledge either of History, or Poetry, or Philosophy ; corresponding, he thought, to the faculties of Memory, Imagination, and Reason. "The sense," he said, "which is the door of the intellect, is affected by individual objects only. The images of these individuals — that is, the impressions received by the sense — are fixed in the memory ; and pass into it, in the first instance, entire as it were, just as they occur. These the human mind proceeds to review, and ruminate on ; and therefore, either simply rehearses them, or makes fanciful imitations

of them, or analyzes and classifies them.
Therefore from these three fountains —
memory, imagination, and reason — flow
these three emanations, history, poesy,
and philosophy; and there can be no
others." First, memory records and stores
up facts. This originates history; and
history is either natural, or civil, each of
which has three subsections. Secondly,
imagination, working on the things of
sense, idealizes them, and originates poetry,
which — according to Bacon — is either
narrative, dramatic, or parabolical. Finally,
the reason working analytically originates
philosophy, "which has three objects, viz.,
God, Nature, and Man." "Nature strikes
the human intellect with a direct ray,
God with a refracted ray, and Man with
a reflected ray;" and so we have "the
doctrine of the Deity, the doctrine of Nature, and the doctrine of Man." The
second and the third of these Bacon subdivided. His doctrine of nature (natural
philosophy) he arranged as speculative,
and as practical; and the speculative he
subdivided into physics and metaphysics, to
which he added mathematics. The doctrine of man he subdivided into human

and civil philosophy ; and under both he placed several minor sciences.

But the Baconian classification is full of flaws. The faculties of memory, imagination, and reason do not stand apart — as Bacon fancied they do — and, working apart, give rise to the several sciences. He held that history arose out of the exercise of the faculty of memory by itself ; but surely the reason, and even the imagination, are quite as much needed as the memory is in the construction of history ? Then even supposing that it was correct to place philosophy amongst the sciences (which it is not), if God, Nature, and Man form a rigid tripartite division, questions will be rediscussed in the third section which really belong to the second. Why should human physiology, *e. g.*, be detached from the general science of physiology ? and again, why should metaphysics be a subsection of the doctrine of nature ? and mathematics be thrown in as a sort of corollary to physics ? There is much arbitrariness in Bacon's arrangement of the provinces of knowledge.

Passing over many noteworthy schemes, we reach that of Hegel. In his *Encyclopæ-*

dia of the Philosophical Sciences we have a
magnificent piece of intellectual work —
solid constructive masonry. Hegel formed
a really grand conception of a universal science, that should include within it the details of all the rest ; and he thought that,
in the experience of the individual and of
the race combined, we reach a knowledge
of the absolute essence both of nature and
of man. In all nature he saw a mirror of
intelligence. Mind was objectified, or so-
lidified, in the external world : Reason had
become incarnate in matter. The root
of everything was the Idea itself ; but
thought had thrust itself forth, objectify-
ing itself in nature ; afterwards, it returned
back to itself, and reached a second
(higher) knowledge in self - consciousness.
The Hegelian division of knowledge thus
became tripartite ; the first section including logic, the second the philosophy of nature, and the third the philosophy of spirit.
Under the second head were included the
sciences of mathematics, physics, and organic life. The third was also subdivided
into three ; the first (or the doctrine of
the subjective spirit) embracing anthropology, phenomenology, and psychology ; the

second (or the doctrine of the objective spirit) including legal right, individual morality, and state morality ; the third (or the doctrine of the absolute spirit) dealing with art, religion, and the absolute philosophy.

The merit of Hegel's classification is that he strove to incorporate the scattered sciences into an organic whole, and to interpret them all, as parts of a universal science to which each was contributory. Its skill was conspicuous, and its suggestiveness great ; but it erred *ab initio*, and is as full of flaws as Bacon's classification was. Hegel's radical blunder was this. He started with an assumption of what the sciences must be, and built them up out of *a priori* notions detached from experience. This was as bad as any of the assumptions of the mediæval philosophy which it discarded. From an *a priori* postulate he endeavored to construct a hierarchy of the sciences one by one. He evolved a solar system out of the abstract ; and, in doing so, broke away from the facts of science, established by Newton. The planets he finds *must* be the most perfect of celestial bodies ; and not being able to account for the fixed stars, he sets them down as mere formal existences, and says that the astral, as compared with the solar, system is as little admirable as a disease of the skin, or a swarm of flies !

A very significant result of the Hegelian system was that the subsequent natural philosophy of Germany, imbibing its spirit, entered for a time on a path of antagonism to the science of the rest of Europe, and intensified the schism between science and philosophy for a generation. If we start with the idea that the visible universe is the outcome of an act of thought on the part of the Infinite mirrored to us in the realm of the finite, it seems natural to conclude that the human mind may think over again the thoughts of the divine, and therefore that the true way to construct the sciences is to evolve them altogether from within. The whole course of history has proved that by no royal road of demonstration can physical science be evolved from an *a priori* postulate, that it is only by the slow and patient induction of facts — by humble experiment, and by tests *a posteriori* — that it can secure its triumphs. The contempt of certain philosophers for the teachings of experience, and their efforts to deduce scientific truth from assumed data, may account for the arrogance with which some of the scientific guides of Europe have decried philosophy; *e. g.*, the bitter way in which Hegel attacked Sir Isaac Newton led to the obvious retort on the part of scientific men that philosophers lived in cloudland.

Leaving Hegel I come to Auguste Comte, who perhaps did more for the positive sciences than any other writer of this century. To Comte science was everything. Philosophy was merely the co-ordination of the results of the separate sciences, or a systematization of the miscellaneous mass of facts and laws which science yields. Thus to him the supreme problem of philosophy was the classification of the sciences. He held that our knowledge extends only to facts, and the relations of facts. What underlies them, what causes them, and what transcends them, is hidden from our faculties. Therefore, phenomena and the laws of phenomena are the alpha and the omega of knowledge. Another central doctrine in his teaching was that the human mind has progressed historically through three

stages : the first, a theological or mytho-
logical stage, in which occult powers were
accepted as the causes of natural phenomena ; the second, a metaphysical stage, in
which abstract essences or substances
were supposed to underly phenomena, and
to explain them ; the third, a scientific or
positive stage, in which only the phenomena themselves and their laws have been
recognized as within the sphere of the
knowable. Comte held that this sequence
of stages is invariably seen in the development of the human mind. As a reading of
history or a generalized law of progress,
however, it is as unverifiable as is Hegel's
a priori doctrine.

Comte proceeded to classify the sciences, in the light of this law of Evolution ;
and at the outset, he laid down a distinction of great value, viz., the distinction between the abstract and the concrete. Abstract science seeks the laws which govern,
and must govern, all phenomena, howsoever
they appear ; laws which are true of those
combinations of phenomena which actually
exist, but which would have been equally
true of any other combinations; *e. g.*, Chemistry tells us of the laws to which all bodies

must conform, while Mineralogy unfolds the conditions under which they actually do appear. Therefore, the former is an abstract, and the latter a concrete science. Again, Biology tells us of the universal laws of life, to which all living creatures must conform ; Botany and Zoölogy unfold the particular conditions of life, to which we find they do conform in the concrete world of experience. We have thus a broad division of the sciences into two main classes — the abstract, which relate to general or universal laws, and the concrete, which deal with particular or special things. It is to the former class that the name Science properly belongs ; the concrete sciences are rather classifications of existing phenomena. They spring up earlier than the abstract sciences, but they are much later in reaching their final form ; because the laws on which they depend, and to which the phenomena conform, are less easily discovered.

It is to the abstract sciences that Comte almost exclusively confined himself. They are the fundamental ones ; and he arranged them in an ascending scale, according as they are respectively general or

special, and according as they depend upon
each other.   Each science depends on the
laws of the science which precedes it, to
which it adds new ones of its own.   He
next finds that the phenomena which form
the basis of the sciences are divisible into
the organic and the inorganic.   The organic
are more complex and less general than
the inorganic.   The former are dependent
upon the latter, and include the latter within
them ; because it is inorganic material that
becomes organized, and the dependence of
the sciences on one another increases, as
the series advances. Inorganic phenomena
are divided into celestial and terrestrial —
the former being more general and independent than the latter.   Thus the science
of astronomy comes first.   Any and every
terrestrial phenomenon is to us more complex than the most intricate of celestial phenomena. The most complex astronomical
problem is really less intricate than the
simplest terrestrial one. Terrestrial physics fall into sections governed by the same
principle.   Chemical phenomena are more
complex than mechanical or physical ones,
chemical action being modified by weight,
heat, electricity, etc.   Therefore physics,

which follows astronomy, precedes chemistry, these three sciences covering the whole realm of the inorganic. Turning to organic phenomena, these present themselves either as relating to the individual, or to the species ; yielding as result the sciences of physiology or biology, and sociology. Thus we have the five affiliated sciences of astronomy, physics, chemistry, biology, and sociology ; the whole series being preceded by another, which is the most radical, the most abstract, and independent of them all, and therefore in a sense preëminent, viz., mathematics.

It is when Comte passes on to consider man, as the highest and the most characteristic of living beings, that he fails, both in his classification and in his results. Man is a microcosm, and sums up in his nature the characteristic features of all creatures underneath him. He is the highest product of organization, or the organized life of the world ; but he is nothing more. Comte does not admit that anything in the cosmos is higher than an organized structure. Mind is merely a function of matter, and therefore the subjective examination of consciousness is delusive.

It leads to nothing. As mind cannot be studied apart from matter, there is no science of psychology, as distinct from physiology. Man is only a highly organized animal, and sociology — or the study of man in the aggregate — is only an extended branch of physiology. In short, the physical absorb the mental sciences within them.

Comte's classification has been sharply criticised by an English disciple of the same school of philosophy, Mr. Herbert Spencer. Spencer's arrangement of the sciences has acquired much celebrity, and his influence over contemporary English thought has been great.

Mr. Spencer's principle of classification is that each class must include within it "those objects which have more characteristics in common with one another than any of them have in common with any objects excluded from the class ; and that those characteristics possessed in common by these objects, and not possessed by other objects, must be more radical than any of the characteristics possessed by them in common with other objects." The broadest natural division among the sciences, he thinks, is the division, first, into those which deal with the abstract relations under which phenomena are presented to us, and, secondly, those which deal with the phenomena themselves. Thus the sciences which deal with Space and Time are separated, by the profoundest of all distinctions, from the sciences which deal with what is disclosed to us in space and time. They treat of the forms in and under which phenomena are known to us; and the two sciences of logic and mathematics belong to this category. Contrasted with these are the sciences which treat of the phenomena themselves; and these fall into two categories, according as we deal with them in their elements, or in their totalities. The latter are the concrete sciences, and they include astronomy, geology, biology, psychology, sociology; the former are abstract-concrete, and they include mechanics, physics, chemistry.

In this there is a partial resemblance to Comte's classification, but Mr. Spencer uses the words abstract and concrete differently from Comte. According to Comte, each science has an abstract part, and a concrete part. According to Mr. Spencer, some sciences are wholly abstract, and others wholly concrete; while others are intermediate, or half of the one and half of the other. To glance briefly at the three. The sciences belonging to the first class deal with relations, and not with realities; with the forms of things, and not with the things themselves. The sciences of the second class deal with realities, but not as they are actually manifested to us, only as these real things are by us artificially separated from one another. The sciences of the third class deal with realities as they actually appear. To the first or abstract class belong logic, which deals with qualities; and mathematics, which deals with quantities. To the second, or abstract-concrete class, belong: first, the sciences which investigate the laws of force, as manifested by matter in masses, such as mechanics, statics, dynamics; and, secondly, the sciences which investigate the laws of force, as manifested by matter in molecules, such as chemistry, the sciences of heat, light, electricity, and magnetism. In all these we carry on an analytical investigation of nature, by decomposing or separating its phenomena. The third, or concrete sciences, take cognizance of the groups of actual phenomena, and aim not at an analytical, but a synthetical treatment of them. They include astronomy, mineralogy, meteorology, geology, biology, psychology, and sociology. These three groups of sciences yield us respectively the laws of the forms, the factors, and the products of nature.

Here again, however, I think there are some radical difficulties. Mr. Spencer's primary distinction between objects and relations — on which his separation of the two abstract sciences of logic and mathematics from the concrete ones is founded — is far from satisfactory ; and, even if it were a true distinction, I do not see that any adequate classification of knowledge could be based upon it, because there is no science within the circle of knowledge that does not deal both with objects and relations. There can be no relations without objects, and all objects have relations each to each. This is but one of several criticisms which might be passed on the Spencerian catalogue, although it is, in many respects, a distinct advance on all previous arrangements of the sciences.

The following classification may perhaps

avoid some of the defects in the schemes criticised, without falling into others equally great. I say perhaps advisedly, because the problem is difficult, and the risk of failure great.

Two things must at the outset be kept in view. First, we must avoid the coinage of new words, with the view of more accurately defining our departments. To affix an uncouth name to a newly discovered section of knowledge is bad enough ; but to recast the old terminology, by which the sciences have been known time out of mind, in favor of some new phrase, is pedantic as well as arbitrary. Such reminting of terms can never yield the current coin of the future. Second, the effort to avoid cross-division may be carried so far as to result in a one-sided classification. A harmonious arrangement of the provinces of knowledge is of course the end we have in view ; at the same time it may be better — while the sciences are still developing — to leave a few unsymmetrical subsections in our scheme, than to attain symmetry by the exclusion of a single province, which cannot be easily fitted into its place.

Two illustrations may now be given of the way in which the sciences might be grouped. Starting with the distinction between Nature and Man, they might be arranged, first, as object-sciences, and, secondly, as subject-sciences; in other words, we might begin with those which concern the outward universe surrounding us, and then take up those which relate to the inward nature of the knower. The former, the object-sciences, might then be subdivided into the organic and the inorganic; each of which would be susceptible of numerous subdivisions. Again, the whole group of the sciences might be arranged, first, as abstract and general, and secondly, as concrete and special; and therefore, to a certain extent the former class would be simple, and the latter complex. In these two samples of classification it will be observed that the former arises out of a distinction between the provinces of knowledge, while the latter is based upon a difference in its characteristics.

I prefer, however, to make the fundamental distinction between the sciences, not that of the abstract and concrete, or the general and special, nor even to distinguish them as the sciences of nature and of man, but rather to divide them thus: First, the sciences including and dealing with the phenomena of *mind;* and, secondly, the sciences including and dealing with the phenomena of *matter.* This root distinction, simple as it is, and possibly just because it is so obvious, will be found to yield a more symmetrical arrangement of the groups than any other.

To begin with the sciences belonging to the former class, there is, first, *Logic,* the science of the phenomena and laws of thought, of reasoning, inference, and evidence. Second, *Psychology,* the science of the phenomena of the human mind, of the senses and the intellect of man. Third, *Ethics,* the science of morality, dealing with the phenomena of the emotions and the will, with the springs of conduct and their outcome. Fourth, *Sociology,* the science which investigates the relation of man to man in the body corporate, the conditions and laws of human welfare, so as to insure the stability of the social organism. (Sociology, it will be seen, touches on political economy, on ethics, and on law.) Fifth, *History*, the science which traces the phenomena and laws of social evolution, illustrated on the field of experience. Sixth, *Jurisprudence*, the science which deals with the principles of law and order, of social contract, and of government ; in other words, the relation in which the units stand to the whole in each nation, and in which nation stands to nation in the larger area of the world. Seventh, *Language*, the science of the various forms of speech, and of their relation one to another. (The sciences of Grammar and of Comparative Philology might perhaps be regarded as subsections of the general science of Language ; the philological structure of any particular language being a distinct province of inquiry from that of comparative philology. Rhetoric belongs to the arts, and has no place amongst the sciences.) Eighth, *Æsthetics*, the science which traverses the whole department of the beautiful, so far as the phenomena of beauty can be reduced to law. Ninth, the science of *Religion*, dealing with the phenomena of the human mind in their relation to that which transcends the finite, and the efforts made by

man to construct a theory of the ways in
which the Infinite manifests itself. All
these sciences are, less or more, sciences of
mind. They have for their subject-matter
the phenomena of mind, as distinct from
the phenomena of matter.

Turning now to the second class, which
includes the sciences dealing with the phenomena of *matter*, I do not of course refer
to crass material substance, but to the
phases which the material world assumes,
the aspects under which it may be regarded, and the laws which can be deduced
from our observation of these. First, at
the base of the series, I place the science
which in a certain sense is a link of connection between the two classes, as it
deals with the quantitative relations of
things, with number and space. It is the
science of *Mathematics*, with its numerous
subsections. Second, *Experimental Physics*, dealing with the laws of matter and
motion, in their complexity and variety;
with its subsections, Statics, and Dynamics, the laws of the phenomena of Light, of
Heat, of Electricity, and of Magnetism.
Third, *Chemistry*, the science which investigates the ultimate constituents of bodies,

and by analysis resolves complex substances into their elements. Fourth, *Astronomy*, the science which deals with the constitution, the laws, and the properties of celestial bodies. Fifth, the science of *Engineering*. Engineering is half a science and half an art; and, on the scientific side, it may be brought under Statics and Dynamics; but, as it deals with the strength of materials, and the laws of construction, it is perhaps better to place it apart by itself. Sixth, *Biology*, the science of the phenomena of life and of living things; which may be subdivided, according as life is seen organized in the two kingdoms of nature, the vegetable and the animal; the result being the two sciences of *Botany* and *Zoölogy*. I need hardly point out that zoölogy has numerous subsections, such as Ornithology, Ichthyology, Entomology, etc. Seventh, *Geology*, the science of the laws by which the present surface of the earth has assumed the form which it now presents. Eighth, *Mineralogy*, the science which deals with the substances that have been shaped by the forces of which geology tells us, the constituent elements of those rock-substances which now diversify the earth.

(It is proper to note that Mineralogy might be considered as a department of chemistry.) Ninth, *Meteorology*, the science which treats of the constitution of the atmosphere and the laws regulative of weather changes, etc. Tenth, the large group of the *Medical Sciences*, which deal with the human organism in health and in disease, with the way of promoting the one and preventing the other. Here, of course, science and art must join hands; we cannot separate the healing art from the science of medicine. In one of the subsections of the group (that, namely, of medical jurisprudence) we also see how the medical and the legal sciences touch each other. The last science, eleventh, which I reserve for this section, is that of *Political Economy*. It deals with the phenomena and the laws of wealth. It traces the causes of the wealth of nations, and investigates the best way of distributing, as well as of producing, wealth. From its close relation to Sociology, however, this science might almost lie between the two groups, as well as be included in the latter of them.

I have not attempted to show how one science gives rise to another, or depends upon it; nor how the sciences bear upon the arts; nor how the theoretical and practical are intertwisted in experience. These questions demand separate treatment in detail.

Some of the advantages, however, to be derived from the attempt to classify our knowledge — even if the effort is only partially successful — may be referred to in conclusion. (1.) If our knowledge is coördinated so that we see how the entire structure is compacted by what each element supplies, we will have a much clearer idea of the function of the separate sciences, as well as of the scope of the whole. (2.) Classification shows us the unity that underlies the diversity of knowledge, the distinctions of the separate sciences being maintained, and yet transcended. The recognition of the inner affinities of knowledge, of its occult correspondences and relations — of the priority of one principle and the subordination of another — must add to the importance of the humblest. (3.) We see how one science helps another, and the extent of the debt they owe to each other. The most important discoveries ever made have been the result of coöpera-

tion — sometimes the unconscious coöpera-
tion — of workers in two or more sciences.
The debt that Geometry owes to Algebra,
that Optics owes to Chemistry (in the discoveries of spectrum analysis, for example),
reacting again on Astronomy, and the way
in which Psychology has been aided by
Physiology, are illustrations of this. It is
also worthy of note that the specialist does
not necessarily advance his science best by
mere specialization. It is rather by bringing one science to bear upon another that
the most notable results have been achieved
and the greatest discoveries made. (4.) An
appreciation of what has been done by
others is one of the best results of a study
of the map of human knowledge. Naturally, we overestimate our own department,
and possibly the best work ever done in
the world would not be done without such
exaggeration. It is well for us, however, to
have some knowledge of the achievements
of those with whose labor in detail we
can never become acquainted. The width
of mental vision, which such a survey gives,
should promote a sort of intellectual free-
masonry ; and that, in turn, should develop
the social friendliness, which lessens the
misunderstandings of life.

ETHICAL PHILOSOPHY AND EV-
OLUTION.

Discipline in Philosophy is at once a great inheritance of academic life, and a permanent necessity of the human intellect. We are to pursue research within a province, which has drawn towards it — — with a singular magnetic spell — the devotion of successive generations. To solve the problems of Philosophy, or to discover the limit of all possible solutions, has been the ambition of every university student from mediæval times. It has been said that in Scotland we all inherit the speculative craving, and that metaphysics are indigenous to our soil. This is but a slight exaggeration of the fact that Philosophy has for centuries formed the centre of our academic discipline, and that we have clothed the venerable word with a meaning which gives it indisputable pre-eminence in the curriculum of a liberal education.

It is the fashion, however, to describe the present age as predominantly scientific, to affirm that the intellectual interest of the hour has drifted away from speculation, and that the surmises of Philosophy have been abandoned for the more sober teachings of experience. With this opinion I am unable to concur. Were it correct, it should be described as a temporary aberration of the human intellect, deserting the " philosophia perennis " in behalf of an empiricism, which — in the sphere of half-truths — is as easily demonstrable, as it is commonplace and crude. But such an interpretation of the spirit of our age is altogether superficial. Far and wide throughout the republic of letters, in Britain, on the Continent, and in America, there are authentic signs of a general *renaissance* of Philosophy. Within the last quarter of a century those speculative problems — which are the theme of perennial debate in the metaphysical schools — have awakened an interest, that is prophetic of a new future for philosophy. There has been a remarkable quickening of the spirit of inquiry into all radical questions, and a far clearer understanding of their issues; while the general mind, both in Europe and America, may be said to be face to face with problems, which, in the last generation, were confined to a few scholars, or recluse speculative men.

It is unnecessary to trace the causes, European or insular, which have led to this result; it is enough to note it as one of the characteristics of our age. Instead of Philosophy being superseded, or submerged in Science, there are indications of a notable reaction in its favor, and of its vigorous pursuit in unexpected quarters. The splendor and rapid march of the physical sciences, which threatened for a time to eclipse if not to extinguish interest in the older problems which lie behind them, has merely opened up fresh pathways converging, as before, on Philosophy as the *scientia scientiarum*; and in the chief tendencies at work at the great educational centres, every one may see the reawakening of speculative thought. The whole literary atmosphere is charged with Philosophy. The leaders of physical research are dealing with metaphysical questions. The topics with which modern science is most engrossed are speculative

ones. In the doctrines of evolution and
transformation of energy we not only find
the revival of old metaphysical theories
under a new scientific dress, but, apart
from philosophy, these questions are still,
as formerly, incapable of solution.   The
recent literature of Philosophy is also rich
in treatises which are greatly in advance
of the contributions of the previous age.
Without naming any particular work or
writer, I may refer to such phenomena
as these : The encounters between the
most accomplished physicists and metaphysicians on ground common to both
(the same problem being approached by
the one from beneath, and by the other
from above) ; the interest awakened in the
problems of sociology ; the light which
has been cast by philosophic criticism
on much that was deemed inexplicable
in the records of the past ; the remarkable development of the historical and
comparative methods of research, as well
as of those purely critical and analytic ;
the attention given to the great masters
of ancient wisdom, especially to the leaders of the Greek schools ; the opening up
of fresh sources of information as to In-

dian and Oriental thought; the establishment of new journals and societies especially devoted to psychological, metaphysical, and ethical study; — these are only a few of the signs of the working of the philosophic spirit, and the revival of speculation in our time. I may add that all the higher poetry and religious literature of the world are saturated with Philosophy as perhaps at no previous period in history. Everywhere inquiry converges on first principles. Even those who abjure metaphysics unconsciously philosophize in their rejection of it; while the subdivision of intellectual labor — due to the growing complexity of culture, and the increasing number of those who devote their lives to research — has widened the area, as well as deepened the lines of investigation.

One result of this diffusion of interest in the questions of Philosophy, and the popularization of its problems, is a better understanding — up to a certain point — of the great rival systems. There is more eclecticism in the intellectual air. It is beginning to be recognized that opinions, which, when fully developed, come into sharp collision with each other, may spring

from a common root of truth ; and that,
in their origin, they may be only a way
of throwing emphasis on this or that side
of a fact that is equally admitted by the
advocates of opposing schools. It is being
seen that no system of Philosophy which
has lived, and won the assent of intellectual men, is entirely false ; and that no one
which has passed away is absolutely true.
Every one now recognizes that the most
perfect system of belief is doomed to extinction, as certainly as the least perfect.
From none can error be eliminated ; and
the longevity of each is mainly due to the
pressure within it of elements that are perennial over those that are accidental and
casual. In the most erroneous, there is
some truth and excellence concealed ;
while, in the most true, error, partiality,
and bias invariably lie hid. In the recognition of this fact is contained the principle of catholicity in thought, and of toleration in practice. The old maxim, that
"every error is a truth abused," remains
the basis of a wise and sober eclecticism.

It is also true that the causes which have
hitherto led to differences of philosophical
opinion are permanent ones, working in

the blood and brain of the race ; and some recent discussions in Philosophy have shown the inveteracy with which the disciples of particular schools continue to interpret facts in their own way, and the strength of the constitutional bias which incapacitates certain minds from seeing both sides of a question.

The causes which differentiate the schools of Philosophy arise at once from the individuality of the system-builders, and from the thousand influences by which each is either consciously or unconsciously affected. The former of these causes is due to remote ancestral tendencies, descending in the line of hereditary succession, from no one knows how distant a fountain-head, as well as to the creative power of the system-builder working in the present hour. The latter may be traced in the education he has undergone, and in the examples that have moulded him from his infancy. Native idiosyncrasy, temperamental bias, and the force of surroundings determine the character of the opinions formed, and the type of the system that results.

It follows that the rigorous logician, in

his dislike of what is vague or paradoxical, will of necessity be unjust to the mystic intuitionalist ; while the latter may fail to appreciate the prosaic love of fact, the demand for verification, the desire that the intellectual firmament should be clear of mist, and that dislike of all nebulous and impalpable theories, which is invariably shown by the disciples of experience. These things must survive in the future, and determine the alternate victory of opposing schools of thought, in much the same way as they influence the sphere of politics. It is as irrational to believe that one particular school (intuitional or experiential, *a priori* or *a posteriori*) will dominate in the future, as it is to suppose that the supremacy of a Conservative Government will be perpetual ; or that, if turned out of office, it will not come back, in due time, with a majority. No political party can remain permanently in power. The same causes that lead to its elevation, tend to its depression, and to the future enthronement of its rival. Similarly, the great pendulum of human thought continues — and must continue — to oscillate throughout the ages ; and the historical succession of opposite schools is inevitable. If the dominant Philosophy in England to-day is the experientialism of Locke, it is certain to be succeeded by a new school of *a priori* ontologists. For as with empires and dynasties, so with systems of opinion, the moment of the greatest triumph is also the moment of the first decline and fall.[1] It is probable, however, that as our historical knowledge becomes more thorough, and we are better acquainted with the philosophies of the past, — especially with the causes that have led to the rise of the great systems, — there will be a more general and adequate appreciation of each ; and that a wise and sober eclecticism, which shuns "the falsehood of extremes," will result. The next great school of British thought will certainly be eclectic, in tone and character if not in name. It may be more profoundly eclectic in spirit, if it is not so in the letter.

It is to be observed, however, that eclectic schools are usually feeble in charac-

---

[1] It is to be noted that the historical succession is equally kept up by the rise of opposite or reactionary theories, as it is by the development of existing opinion. Intellectual progress is often due to antagonistic reaction, and the reappearance of discarded theories.

ter, and barren in result, and that they often collapse before the renewed vigor of some sectarian movement. It cannot be denied that there has been a want of inner coherency in many of them ; and if they are the offspring of compromise, or consist in a mere miscellaneous piecing together of the details of opposite systems, — so that the result is an artificial patchwork, or at best an intellectual mosaic, — no other result than sterility is possible.

The nature of Philosophy, as distinguished from ordinary knowledge, will best be understood through a series of contrasts, which lead up to the main characteristic difference. The first distinction is between a liberal and a professional education; the second, the distinction between the objective and the subjective in knowledge; the third, between the seeming and the real; the fourth, between science and philosophy.

In the light of these distinctions, we shall see that it is the aim of Philosophy to escape from the illusions of inherited or acquired belief, that it may reach the ultimate ground of human knowledge; and this may be further described as either an ascent above, or a descent beneath, our secondary opinions to the region of first principles. We shall see that its aim is to reach the permanent and abiding, as contrasted with the incessantly changing aspects of phenomenal existence; and that its function is to get behind all the metaphoric modes of thought, or pictured representations of reality, to the reality itself which pictures and symbols represent. The common consciousness of mankind is in bondage to the concrete and the pictorial. It sees essence only in the light of symbol, and confuses the two together. Philosophy distinguishes them, and conducts from the symbol to the thing symbolized; while it seeks the one ultimate ground of all detached and fragmentary knowledge. It is the quest for that supreme unity, in the vision of which the separateness and detail of miscellaneous knowledge is lost to view. Thus Philosophy teaches that beyond the customary and traditional, behind the pictorial and concrete, within the changing, and beneath the miscellaneous, lies the sphere of the true, the real, the sempiternal, and the one.

Having ascertained what it is we are to

study, — with its uses, and its place in the curriculum of a liberal education, — we must next determine on the method to be pursued in our inquiries. These questions, however, are merely preliminary, leading up to the specific problem of *ethics*. It is not Philosophy in general but Moral Philosophy in particular that is to be studied by us ; and its sphere and province may be defined in either of two ways.

In the first place, we may consider it in its relation to, and in its distinction from, the other branches which grow out of the common root of human knowledge, such as science, theology, politics, and æsthetics. Its sphere and its boundaries cannot be accurately known, till they are known in the light of those relations, which connect it inseparably with the provinces which border it, on the right hand and on the left. For example, it is organically related to psychology. It is vitally connected with theology. It is indissolubly allied to sociology. It has a close relation to physiology. And yet, on the other hand, ethics has repeatedly suffered from undue encroachment by each of these correlated departments of knowledge. Now, it has been regarded as an appendix or subsection of psychology; again, it has been sunk in metaphysic, the distinction between the psychology and the metaphysic of ethics being ignored. It has been regarded as a simple corollary to our knowledge of the phenomena of organization: that is to say, it has been sunk in physiology. It has also been described as a province once independent, but now conquered and annexed by the Christian religion. These are illegitimate curtailments or suppressions. And the penalty of trespass, by any recognized body of knowledge upon the domain of another, is always a weakening of the enlarged province, which is made too wide by its attempted annexation of another. As, in the political history of a people, the conquest of alien states and the annexation of distant territory are the invariable prelude to national disaster — as they lead to the breaking up of the kingdom that has overgrown, or of the commonwealth that has become too vast — so, in the realm of knowledge, a "lengthening of cords" is not always accompanied by a corresponding "strengthening of stakes."

At present the chief encroachment on the sphere of Ethics comes from the side of physical science, or physiology. In the last generation it frequently came from the side of religion : that is to say, many English writers supposed that the function of what they called "natural ethics," as distinguished from "revealed morality," was gone. To the question, whether the rules of conduct, discoverable by reason and intuition, or gathered by experience, were valid guides to action, it was replied that they were not; because Christianity had taken the place of natural morality, and superseded it. This distinction, however, is invalid. What is "natural" cannot be superseded. It cannot even be placed in a category opposite to what is "revealed." The real distinction and contrast is between what is natural, and what is artificial. The fact that anything has been "revealed" merely implies that it was previously unknown, or lay in shadow; and the disclosure of every truth, however it may happen to have come to light, is, strictly speaking, a revelation. Its simple occurrence has all the force of a revelation, whether it belongs to the sphere of morals or religion. We shall see, as our course proceeds, how the one province is indebted to the other; and how, by the spirituality of its ideal, Christianity has given the human race a moral leverage in the pursuit of virtue unknown to the ancient schools. But it is equally necessary to vindicate the integrity and independence of ethics, as it is to point out how far, and in what directions, it is beholden to religion.

The second method, by which the sphere of ethics may be defined, is by a condensed summary of its chief problems, which may be presented in the form of answers to the following questions : (1.) What are the facts of man's moral nature? how are we constituted, and endowed, as moral agents? (2.) How has human nature come to be what it is? out of what prior conditions or elements has it emerged? In other words, what are the causes or forces — individual and social, temperamental and racial — that have determined the moral development of humanity, and working in unison have fashioned the destiny of each agent? The "natural history" of morals will be treated under this head, or the growth of ethical ideas out of their rudi-

mentary types; and the curious phases
which the moral consciousness has undergone in the course of its evolution will be
discussed. (3.) What ought man morally to
be? The contrast between the actual and
the ideal, between human aspiration and
attainment, with the authority of conscience, and the nature of free will, fall to
be considered under this head. (4.) How
can human nature attain to its ideal, and
be brought into practical accordance with
law and order? By what power or process
can moral harmony be reached, the discord
of the powers abolished, and the ethical
ideal be made real, in experience? In
other words, how can man reach his destiny? Under this fourth head of inquiry
the relation between Ethics and Religion
comes again to be considered.

Having answered these four questions in
detail, the great systems of Moral Philosophy, ancient and modern, must be historically and critically discussed. The stream
of ethical opinion must be followed from
the Greek schools onwards, with the view
more especially of exhibiting the genealogy
of doctrine, and the " increasing purpose "
of the various systems. At the close of

this investigation we shall return to the phenomena of the moral consciousness, and ask, what are the inferences deducible from it, or its implicates, as to the divine nature, and the destiny of the human soul? Thus, our ethical inquiries will naturally lead to theology and religion.

From this brief preliminary outline, it will be seen that it is the phenomena of human character which, in the first instance, supply the ethical student with his field of observation. The area of that field is a wide one. It includes all our desires and affections, the emotions and the will, with the practical activities and developed habits which are the outcome of character. It embraces all that exists, and is evolved, within the plastic region of human conduct, — a region various and manifold, at times heterogeneous and occult. We begin with an investigation of the facts of consciousness. We proceed thence to an historical inquiry as to the process of development by which these facts have come to be what they now are. This leads to the further question of the meaning of duty (a speculative problem), and to the conduct of life (a practical discipline).

In its most comprehensive aspect, then, Moral Philosophy has two sides. From its connection with human knowledge, and from the necessity of our having an intellectual root or ground of action, it is a speculative study. From its connection with conduct, and the necessity of our realizing in life and action the principles of which it seeks the explanation, it is a practical discipline. As a body of knowledge it stretches between theory and practice, and is the arch which spans the chasm connecting speculation and action. On one side, it is the theory of our practice; on the other, it is the practice of the theory we adopt. Speculatively considered, it is a systematized body of knowledge dealing with human conduct. Its aim is to explain the nature and to determine the rationale of duty. It considers man, however, not merely as a knower and contemplator, but also as an actor; as a practical being whose conduct is susceptible of direct regulation and indirect control. Ascertaining the laws which govern character, it essays an explanation of habit. Endeavoring to unfold the relation between conduct and welfare, it distinguishes while it connects duty and happiness. So far as it confines itself within the region of facts, it is simply a branch of psychology. It is ethical psychology, or the psychology of the moral, as distinguished from the intellectual consciousness. When, however, we ask the meaning of duty, or seek the rationale of conduct, we transcend the phenomenal sphere. Our inquiry becomes a speculative one. Rising into the metaphysic of ethics, it is ontological rather than scientific.

To put it otherwise, we stand in certain definite relations to our fellow-men, as members of the same social organism, and definite duties follow or flow from these relations. So long as we investigate these, dealing with them merely as facts, in order that we may discover the laws which underlie the phenomena, — facts of which the phenomena are the expression, and the laws the explanation, — we are simply studying what happens, and the manner of its happening. But the moment we raise the further question of the meaning of duty, and, perceiving that there is a frequent contrariety between what we are and what we ought to be, ask *why* we ought to be other than we are, or have been, then we have left the region of moral psychology, and entered that of the metaphysic of ethic. We experience a strife between desire and duty, between appetite and reason ; and, in asking its explanation, the philosophy of morals emerges. In our early years of objectivity and unreflectiveness no such inquiry is ever raised by us; nor is it then needed. What is, what happens — the actual and the existing — satisfies us ; or, if it does not, we seek satisfaction simply by a change in our circumstances and surroundings. Gradually, however, there comes to all of us a sense of imperfection and inadequacy. We are haunted by a feeling of the unattained, while we have occasional glimpses of an ideal that is at once above us, and within our reach. As soon as this is perceived, it acts like a whetstone to our inquiries into the meaning or rationale of duty. The mere register of moral phenomena no longer satisfies us. The record of particular subjective states, simple or complex, — of desires as phenomenal causes, or emotions as phenomenal effects, — cannot satisfy the speculative craving that has been awakened. Detail of that kind is now regarded merely as a collection of preliminary data, which may serve as the raw material for a philosophy of morals.

I thus distinguish between ethical science and ethical philosophy. Philosophy is not a department of science, nor is science a branch of philosophy. Their provinces are distinct, though closely related at their frontier margins. Ethical science deals with the phenomena of our moral nature in all their length and breadth ; ethical philosophy deals with the inner essence of these facts, in its height and in its depth, as well as with the link which connects them indissolubly together. Science treats of the coexistences and succession of phenomena, and of the laws which may be generalized from them. It does not attempt to reach the substrate underlying the phenomena, or the nexus by which they are united. Philosophy pursues both the substrate and the nexus. In so doing, it seeks the ultimate meaning of the whole, as a unity ; and it will not relinquish its search, though science may affirm that its quest is as vain as the pursuit of the sangreal. Starting from the facts of experience, it seeks a theory of these facts. It deduces inferences, which the phenomena do not yield by way of generalization, but by way of necessary implication, or as causes requisite to account for effects otherwise unexplainable.

Thus, to sum up, we may distinguish between the science of morals and the philosophy of duty, as we distinguish the psychology of cognition from the philosophy of knowledge, or the science of taste from the philosophy of the beautiful. In each case, psychology precedes, and metaphysic succeeds.

The usual distinction between metaphysic and ethic is the source of an illusion. If there is a "metaphysic of ethic," the two spheres are not independent of each other, but the one is the root of the other; that is to say, the metaphysical inquiry is an inquiry into the root or ground of the ethical phenomena; just as, in another province, the metaphysical inquiry concerns the root of intellectual phenomena, and as in a third region it deals with the ground of all æsthetic phenomena. They are related as the porch or vestibule is related to the shrine. I would thus classify, as three separate provinces, the Science of knowledge, of duty, and of taste ; setting over against these respectively the three kindred, and co-related though independent, departments of the Philosophy of knowledge, of duty, and of taste. This is, however, to anticipate what it will be the aim of subsequent discussion to make apparent.

It may be rash to express an opinion as to the precise point which Ethical Philosophy has reached in the ever-advancing stream of speculation. This, with a statement of *desiderata*, or problems that await solution, may fittingly be postponed. It is meanwhile more important to note the bearing of the doctrine of Evolution on the origin of the moral faculty ; a question of frequent debate in the ethical schools, — one not unknown to antiquity, nor unsuccessfully handled before the rise of modern scientific method, — but which has come more prominently to the front in the recent literature of philosophy.

Before, however, we can estimate the bearing of the doctrine of Evolution on ethics, we must have a precise idea of the doctrine itself. It has been alleged that if the general principle of development be established, its application to the sphere of morality is only a matter of detail; and that the derivation of all the moral life and consciousness of the race, out of elements originally non-moral, is no longer an hypothesis, but is a fact scientifically known. In order to estimate the value of this assertion, we must first see to what the doctrine amounts, and what is the evidence in its favor.

Experience, individual and collective, shows that every organism and every character alters by minute and imperceptible changes, that each is incessantly varying, that its very life is a series of changes. Further, every living organism, as it gives rise to others, transmits an altered structure, and originates a change of type. So much is within the easily verifiable range of experience, and even of commonplace observation. The theory of development further suggests that we may account for all the differences which now exist in the scale of Nature, the immense varieties of organic phenomena, by a slow succession of similar changes, indefinitely prolonged in ever-varying circumstances, each one imperceptibly minute. Thus it will be seen that the doctrine, fully carried out, abolishes the distinction between genera and species, as well as the difference between species and individuals, all of these being merely conventional distinctions. They are the names which conveniently mark off organisms one from another, when the process of evolution has gone so far, and been in operation so long, that its divergencies require to be signalized in detail, and described at various points. The whole series, having been rigidly developed out of antecedent elements, and continuing still to develop, the notion of independent types disappears. All is process; the products are simply processes prolonged. What is reached at any one stage, however, is necessarily evanescent. Nothing can exist for all time. Each exists for its own time, and perishes, only to make way for an equally perishable successor.

Now, if we cannot suppose that any organisms spring up *de novo*, without natural ancestry, and that any arrive on our earth as foreigners from another planet, whence can they severally spring? If we

exclude spontaneous generation and foreign arrival, we have but two possible theories. Either all have always existed in
some form or other and are only undergoing a series of transformations in time;
or each has been developed out of a different and lower stage, in the incessant com-
petition and struggle for existence. The
present indefinite complexity of organic
forms may be explained, either by the eternal existence of an indefinite number of
fixed ideal types, which are revealing themselves in the varieties of concrete existence, or by the incessant evolution of one
protean principle, which in the transformation of life is assuming endlessly varied
phenomenal forms.

We may safely assume that the physical miracle of the creation of new types,
whether in the form of the spontaneous
generation of minute organisms, or the
sudden appearance of creatures more
highly organized, is not now taking place,
spasmodically. If we had reason to believe that it had ever happened, we
should have equal reason to conclude that
it was occurring perpetually, that the miracle never ceased; which would, in turn,

abolish its miraculous or exceptional character. If, however, it is rash to affirm that nothing can possibly originate, — in the form of organized material structure, —*per saltum*, it is not rash, but only the dictate of a cautious philosophy, to affirm that, since we have no experience of origination in this way, we are not at liberty to assume that it has ever taken place. Unless we discover phenomena that can be explained *in no other way*, — phenomena which remain irreducible and inexplicable as the result of the slow modification of ages, — we have no scientific right, or philosophical warrant, for assuming any break in the process of orderly development by law. So far, then, antecedent presumption, grounded on experience, is in favor of evolution. Evolution is the rule within human experience. Origination *per saltum* is not even an exception to the rule. It is a hypothesis called in to explain the absence of connecting links between the species that exist, the differentiation of organic types, and the remoteness from one another of the individuals which illustrate these types.

Our choice, therefore, does not lie between a doctrine of continuous evolution from a common fountain-head and a doctrine of successive originations at intervals of creative activity, repeated throughout the ages in linear series, — the protoplastic power starting into action after a long period of slumber, and again retiring to rest. The latter notion must be laid aside, as inconsistent with any elevated, not to say reverential, idea of the creative Power that works in nature. Our choice really lies between a doctrine of continuous activity and unceasing development (all things emanating from a single Source, and being the outcome of a solitary principle, endlessly manifesting itself in an indefinite variety of forms); and a doctrine of fixed types, or eternal essences, like the "archetypal ideas" of Plato, which have always existed, and are indestructible types, which emerge and reëmerge — are born, die, and reappear — in the incessant change and palingenesia of the universe.

I do not think that the theory of evolution in organic nature has been *proved*; but it has been rendered the almost inevitable conclusion of the scientific intellect, dealing inductively with the facts of biology (especially of embryology) and palæontology. I do not speak of any particular theory of "natural selection" or "heredity," but of the general doctrine of evolution as opposed to cataclysmic bursts of energy. The protoplasm of the nettle, of the mollusk, of the lizard, and of man is chemically the same. The rise in complexity of structure, from the lowest organism to man, is not greater or more striking than the series of changes through which each individual passes normally from the embryonic to the adult state. The intermediate stages between the lowest form of vitality and the highest are successively reached by all the maturer organisms, so that we may see the ascending scale of animated nature mirrored and summarized in the evolution of every embryo. Now, the marvel to human intelligence, in the development of a feathered fowl out of the albumen of an egg, is not intrinsically greater than the evolution of all the flora and fauna of the universe would be, supposing it to proceed from a common protoplasmic germ. We know that the one takes place incessantly. Its mystery is forgotten, in its constancy and commonness. The other is unknown to experience; but there is no obstacle to

it, in the nature of things. It contains
no greater mystery than the former, and
its future demonstration would not excite
surprise.   Even within the range of experience, we can see development in progress.
Alike in the animal and vegetable kingdoms, amongst the foraminifera and the
diatoms, change and transformation, *within
a limited field*, may be observed ; and the
development of higher organisms out of
lower ones is only an inductive inference,
drawn by analogy, from the phenomena
that fall under our observation, and can be
experimentally investigated.   Even the line
between the animal and the vegetable cannot now be drawn with the rigor by which
the naturalists of the last generation used
to separate the kingdoms of Nature ; while
modern biology will in all likelihood demonstrate the actual emergence of fresh types
of organization out of rudimentary ones.
In this there will be no surprise to science.

It is to be noted, however, that the discovery of a palæontological form, intermediate between man and the ape, would not
prove that man was physically the descendant of such an intermediate ; nor would
it greatly aid the controversy, except as

affording a new link in the chain of organized existence. The theory of evolution will not be demonstrated even by a discovery of *all* the missing links in the chain of existence, but only by a scientific use of the links which we possess, and by warrantable inferences from them.

Does the vital, however, in any instance proceed from the non-vital? Is the boundary between the animate and the inanimate as precarious as that which separates the animal from the vegetable? This ulterior question, which is one of the gravest philosophical import, must arise, even supposing that the derivation of all the varieties of vital existence from one another were a demonstrated conclusion of science. The evolution of nature may be a fact, — a daily and hourly apocalypse; but certainly we have, as yet, no evidence of the non-vital passing into the vital. Spontaneous generation is an imaginative guess, unverified by scientific tests. And matter is not itself alive. Vitality, whether seen in a single cell of protoplasm, or in the human brain, is a thing *sui generis,* distinct from matter, and incapable of being generated out of matter.

The theory, however, that all the higher organized life of the universe has arisen by evolution out of lower forms — although the material never gives rise to the mental, or the non-vital to the vital — seems much more tenable than the counter-theory to which I have referred, namely, that there is within the universe a fixed but indefinitely vast number of distinct types, corresponding to the eternal ideas of Plato, each of which is imprisoned within its own domain, and is kept up by inheritance and succession only within its limited area.

It should be noted that those who explain the rise of every new organized product by simple evolution demand for the accomplishment of the process a length of time that is almost inconceivably vast. It is affirmed by their opponents that the present universe carries within it the signs of a comparatively recent origin, and that it is traveling at no distant date (though it may be measured by millions of years) to extinction ; so that its beginning and its ending are alike evidenced by, and involved in, its present state. This affirmation rests on evidence that is probably quite hidden to one who is not a specialist in physical science. Certainly, if either the unscientific or the speculative mind is to receive it, it must be received on trust. No evidence appreciable by the ordinary mind has been advanced to prove such a limited duration to the existing matter of the universe, or of the globe we inhabit, as to render the evolution of all its organized products impossible within the period.

Let us suppose, however, the fact of evolution to be proved, and every missing link in the chain of derivation to be supplied, the question would remain, *From what is the whole series evolved?* If the higher is evolved from the lower, as a fowl is from the egg, and the man from the child, from what is the lower derived? What started the whole process of derivation? If no hiatus is permissible between any link in the chain of organization, whence did the first in the series proceed? Suppose that, in our regress towards the beginnings of life, we have reached the lowermost step of the descending scale, are we at liberty to suppose a hiatus in the orderly development, millions of ages ago, when the first

germs of vitality started into being? Did
the vital proceed by a still remoter development from the non-vital? or, was it
created by a fiat of volition? or, *has it always existed in some form or other as an
eternal constituent of the universe?* I do
not see how we can escape from the last
alternative. The first is the evolution
theory in its completest form, which as-
signs a material origin to all spiritual phenomena. The second is quite as arbitrary,
if it be thrust into the series of evolving
phenomena far back in the process, — at
an imaginary creative epoch in the morning of time, — as it is when capriciously
introduced between the links of the causal
nexus now. The supposition that it is
more likely to have taken place in a distant age than at present is like relegating
the age of miracle to an imaginary mythic
time, when earth was nearer heaven than
now, and so degrading the idea. We are the
victims of metaphoric illusion in supposing
instantaneous creation to be one whit easier "in the beginning" than now. If time
has had no "morning" and will have no
"evening," creation is as real at the present
moment as it ever was. The notion that

theism is inconsistent with a belief in the eternity of matter has proceeded from the fear that, with matter eternally provided, Deity would have less to do; or that the instantaneous summoning of the raw material of the universe out of non-existence was necessary to prove his omnipotence. But with eternal matter and eternal life, the superintendence of the universe, and the building up of the organized forms which have successively appeared, would require the pervading presence of an *Opifex mundi*, no less than if the matter itself had been created by him. If matter be not eternal, its first emergence into being is a miracle, beside which all others dwindle into absolute insignificance. But, as has often been pointed out, the very process is unthinkable; the sudden apocalypse of a material world out of blank nonentity cannot be imagined; its emergence into order out of chaos, when "without form, and void" of life, is merely a poetic rendering of the doctrine of its slow evolution.

Theism has nothing to fear, but much to gain, from a scientific doctrine of evolution. Behind the proof of the gradual development of life lies the question of its

origin and its Evolver ; and so long as
evolution cannot give a material answer to
the question, *whence came the force* that
gave to matter its first impulse towards
the development of organic life, it is
powerless to suggest, far less to establish,
any atheistic doctrine.   On the other hand,
the evolution of organic life is the grand-
est conceivable illustration of the working
of divine agency not detached from, but
inseparably upbound with, the life of the
universe.   Those who explain the present
cosmical order, and all the varieties of existing organization by development, virtually see in it the disclosure or "revelation"
of several divine attributes, while they affirm that their

faith is large in time,
And that which shapes it to a perfect end.

Thus, the truth of the principle of evolution — not as explanatory of the origin,
but of the procession and development of
material forms — may be conceded, without peril to any verifiable truth of theology.

Is it equally relevant as an explanation
of the phenomena of character, and the
mysteries of our intellectual and moral

being? Can we account for all the varieties in the practice of the race, as the progressive development of tendencies originally very different, but which have undergone modification and change during thousands of generations, and in the course of millions upon millions of experiments? Or do we meet with phenomena within the moral sphere, which are inexplicable by such an extension of the theory of evolution,

– phenomena which are better explained by another hypothesis, and which are irreducible under the all-embracing unity of the former? This is our inquiry now.

In the first place, the fact that the intellectual and moral consciousness of the race has grown or been developed from lower and even dissimilar states must be as frankly conceded, as the rise and development of material organization is conceded. The facts which prove and illustrate this process of growth form a most interesting chapter in the history of human progress. They are indeed a summary of civilization itself. But our inquiry lies behind such an induction of historical facts and instances, however complete and satisfactory it might be made.

In the second place, we have to examine *the nature of the process* of evolution more carefully. Suppose that the present verdicts of the moral consciousness have been evolved out of lower ones, may not the process be more accurately described as one of *emergence*, than as one of creation by development? May not the "increasing purpose" of human history be an increasingly accurate interpretation or reading of the reality of things? In a process of evolution all the stages are of equal value and significance. The very terms "high" and "low," "advanced" and "immature," have no significance, except one that is relative to the insight of the individual who uses them. A standard of intrinsic worth there is none. Hence it is that an experiential theory of the origin of knowledge and of morals fits into a doctrine of evolution ; and conversely, the psychological facts that suggest a non-experiential theory of knowledge and of morals are amongst the most formidable difficulties in the way of the doctrine of evolution. It is true that a perception of the *a priori* or non-experiential character of knowledge, in any of its forms, — as it dawns gradually on the mind of the child, — arises out of a lower state of confused subjective groping. But the lower state does not generate the higher. With the unconscious awakening of intelligence there is a more accurate apprehension of the facts of existence, and a progressive approach is made to a knowledge of the essence and reality of things. It is altogether unwarrantable, however, to affirm that, if we go back to the beginning of things, we may assume that all that now is human lay potentially, if not in embryo, within the primitive ascidian ; that there was a time when intelligence and morality were not, and that these are " things of yesterday " within the slow evolving universe. That the lower contained the higher within it is a gratuitous assumption. It would be more consistent to say that the higher did not exist *at all*, until it came upon the stage of being. This would involve the assumption of a new creation — the very assumption from which evolution seeks to free us. It is surely more philosophical, to suppose that when a new organism appears, its differentia is not due to anything that was latent in its progenitor, but to a fresh development of the

prolific life of the universe, issuing orderly
and incessantly from the fountain-head of
existence, and taking shape moment by
moment in new forms of organization.

There is a further obstacle in the way
of our admitting the unrestricted sway of
evolution within the sphere of intellectual
life and moral agency. If it is difficult to
see how the knowledge of *a priori* truths
can be derived from mere sensation, it is
still more difficult to see how moral freedom can be developed out of necessity.

I do not now enter on the great controversy as to the nature of free-will. The
question of the ages is not to be discussed
in a paragraph. But this much may be
said : if we have evidence to warrant the
belief in moral autonomy, — in such a freedom as constitutes the individual a morally
creative cause, while the causal nexus is
maintained in its integrity, — it is clear
that this freedom cannot be itself " the
creature of circumstances." Evolution and
necessitarianism go hand in hand. They
are different ways of expressing the same
thing. If human nature is wholly evolved,
man is at best a cunningly devised machine,
an automaton. He is what he is, exclu-

sively because of what other things have been, and because of what they have made him. It is unnecessary to indicate the nature of the evidence we have for a transcendental freedom. But it is clear that if evolution contains the whole truth on this subject, if there is no complementary or balancing truth on the other side, moral freedom must be renounced. On the other hand, if moral freedom be a fact, it is a singularly stubborn one, which will neither bend nor fit into a sectarian theory of evolution.

If necessity and automatism be true, and if the evolving stream of tendency be competent of itself to perform the feat of educing all the moral life of the universe out of elements that are originally non-moral, the evidence should be accessible to the unbiased student of the problem. Why should we distrust our moral intuitions, and accept the materialist solution of our genealogy, unless the evidence be overwhelmingly clear, and cogent? It does not appeal to us with any evidence *clare et distincte*, as Descartes would have it. On the contrary there is an *a priori* presumption against it, in the explicit testimony of

consciousness to the power of moral origination.   *Why* am I to believe that a material condition of the molecules of the brain
is the cause of a state of consciousness, and
not to believe that a state of consciousness
can ever be an originating cause of change
in the molecules of the brain?   There is
action and reaction between the material
and the mental.   But it is not an equally
necessitated action and reaction.   It is not
reciprocal, in the sense that both are solely
determined by their antecedents.   The spe-
ciality of the action of the human will and
consciousness lies in their spontaneity and
freedom.

The growth of ethical sentiment and
dogma out of prehistoric elements, during
the innumerable eras of past existence,
must be admitted to be as certain as is the
progress of each individual from the blank
consciousness of childhood to the adult
state ; and the authority of the developed
product is not invalidated by its history
being traced, and the entire series of the
steps of its development disclosed.   That
human character should grow, as well as
the physical organism to which it is related, is merely a corollary of its existence.

That it should have come to be what it is by a process of development is not only no disparagement to it, but is absolutely essential to its existence in any form whatever. Change and development are twin sisters.

For the same reason, it is self-evident that what is now adult in the race, having once been rudimentary, the language of its maturity must be totally unlike the lispings of its infancy. This fact, however, and even the discovery of the precise law or process of its development, does not fully explain the progress, because it casts no light on the nature of the Cause that has determined the advance, or the propelling force that has regulated the evolution. After all our scientific and historical facts are ascertained, the philosophical question remains, Whence, or out of what prior elements, have the moral faculty and the moral feelings been developed? Some of those who find in evolution an adequate explanation of all the problems of philosophy seem to imagine that by simply affirming the *growth* of ethical sentiment and idea, they have solved the puzzle of their origin. Let the fact of development be granted, — not as an argumentative concession, but as an elementary and almost self-evident postulate, — the question still remains, Did the immature give rise to the more mature, or merely go before it? Did the inferior originate the superior, or simply precede it in time?

That the higher succeeded the lower is evident ; but it does not follow that it sprang out of it, in such a way that all the actual and potential elements of its life may be said to have been latent or contained within the lower. The phenomena of simple succession do not explain a single occurrence ; and the fact that a progress is seen from inferior forms to superior types in Nature does not explain the cause of the rise, or assign a reason for the advance. That the cause is contained within the phenomena themselves, and is not due to a force, distinct from the phenomena though inseparable from them, and pervading the entire series — is a dogmatic appendix, which the experience-philosophy superadds to the facts which it experientially investigates.

Merely to affirm that the moral faculty has grown unconsciously in the race, as it grows in the conscious life of each man, is not to make a great discovery in morals, but to state a commonplace which every ethical school admits; although the intuitional moralists may not have perceived its extent so clearly, or admitted its significance so fully, as their rivals have done. To affirm that because it is developed it is also derived from the elements that foster its development is the illicit inference which the derivative moralists either add to, or confound with, the admitted fact.

Because the consciousness of the child is a seeming blank, his mind — to use the old illustration — like a sheet of white paper on which impressions are gradually imprinted from without, was the ground on which the experiential philosophers of the past denied that there were any latent elements within it or behind, which experience did not create, but only evolved, or brought to light. Within the present generation the controversy has merely widened out, from the individual to the race. The genesis of all the faculties is now sought through a wider investigation of prehistoric conditions, and the subsequent struggle for

existence. But it is only the area whence
the inference is deduced that has been
changed. The process of deduction remains the same. If there was anything to
warrant the old contention that what is developed in the individual is not the simple
product of experience, — the mind of the
infant being more like a palimpsest than an
unwritten parchment, — precisely the same
contention is valid now, in reference to the
larger and slower evolution of the historical consciousness of the race. The controversy of to-day is really the old controversy between Socrates and Protagoras,
between Plato and Aristotle, between Leibnitz and Locke, between Kant and Hume,
"writ larger," — through the amazing development of physical science, biological
research, and the prehistoric archæology
of our time. That the ingenious theories
of the teachers of evolution have filled
up for us the possible outlines of a most
interesting chapter in prehistoric archæology is undoubted. The psychological
facts which Darwin has signalized are important factors in the ethical development
of the race; but he has not solved the
ethical problem, and no amount of success-

ful labor, along the lines in which he and his successors have worked, will solve it.

I admit that, were it proved that the moral faculty was derived as well as developed, its present decisions would not necessarily be invalidated. The child of experience has a father whose teachings are grave and peremptory. An earth-born rule may be as stringent, though it is not so august, as one derived from a celestial source. It does not even follow that a belief in the material origin of spiritual existence — accompanied by a corresponding decay of belief in immortality — must *necessarily* lead to a relaxation of the moral fibre of the race. It is certain that it has often done so; but it is equally certain that there have been individuals, and great historical communities, in which the absence of the latter belief has neither weakened moral earnestness, nor prevented devotional fervor. It is clear, therefore, that we should no more discredit what has come to be what it is by a process of development than we should distrust the verdicts of the moral faculty, because future experience may on many points enlarge or widen them. It may even be said that the

derivation of a faculty out of elements originally unlike itself, bringing with it the authority of accumulated experience, indicates
the working of a great cosmic law which
gathers force from the width of the area it
sweeps, and the time it has taken to evolve
its products.   It comes to us now with the
prestige of a remote antiquity, it can appeal to the precedent of a million generations ; and, since it has alone survived in
the struggle for existence, it is fortified in
its appeal by the failure of every rival that
has for a time competed with it, but been
gradually thrust aside.

If this be conceded, we must note with
accuracy what it is we have reached and
found. We observe a continued advance in
the ethical conceptions of the race ; but we
discover no fixed standard of action, no
immutable canon, and hence no absolute
criterion of morality. Since the human race
is still changing and developing, fresh alterations will be produced, by the "increasing purpose" of time, in the moral conceptions and feelings of the race, as certainly
and inevitably as changes on the earth's
surface will be produced by physical agents.
If we have no principle other than evolu-

tion to guide us, nothing underneath the linear series of changes which we call development, which gives to these their character and explanation, we are able to call one thing "good," and another "evil," only because the forces that sway society have happened to develop in one direction, and not in another. I do not say that they might have as easily tended in a direction different from the one they have taken. The fact that only one has been taken, after the myriad struggles of the race, may be held as proof that, to a human nature such as ours, one only was possible. But, on the theory of evolution, the goal is not yet reached. There not only may but there must be endless future development. We have not attained to anything higher than a temporary and therefore a conventional rule of expedient action. An absolute standard is impossible. Since our humanity itself is in a perpetual process of "becoming," its rule of action always "about to be," never absolutely "is." It is essentially relative, necessarily contingent, incessantly changing. What is valid for the human race to-day *may* cease to be valid to-morrow, and *must* cease to be valid in the long run. It will become obsolete through the slow procession of the ages, and the stealthily superannuating hand of time. Can a rule which thus disintegrates and dies away command the reverential suffrage of the race, even while it lasts? Its permanence in any one form being momentary — its deepest characteristic being its incessant change — it may be questioned if we can ever really know what we are asked to reverence.

All "becoming" tends to "being" as its end, or it is meaningless; and we can only explain "becoming" by presupposing "being." If, therefore, what we have to explain is always about to be, but never actually is, — if it is all process and no product, or if the product is simply process prolonged forever, — there is no intelligible meaning in the process itself. Its very rationality disappears. In other words, some knowledge of the end is necessary to give rationality to the means. It is the goal that makes the race intelligible, the port to which the vessel is bound that explains the voyage. In any case, we must have a starting-point and an ending place; two termini, to mark out the course and differentiate it, else the intermediate stages are unintelligible. But, while we cannot get within sight of these termini by the inductions of experience, — whether by an imaginative regress to the fountain-head of history, or by a surmise of its destination, — we find them disclosed and explained at every stage of the intermediate journey, in the consciousness of a law that is autocratic, universal, and ideal.

Not that we can discern the beginnings of morality, or anticipate the development to which it may attain. Even were such surmises or forecasts possible, they would be of no use as data towards the solution of the problem, inasmuch as they would be either gathered historically from the field of experience, or inductively inferred by the aid of analogy. What we reach, however, transcends experience, without being independent of it; nay, by the very help and teaching of experience, we outsoar it.

The chief point to be noted, in connection with a derivative theory of morals, is the position in which it all leaves us in the exercise of moral approbation and disapprobation. On the principle of evolution, all the phases through which ethical opinion and sentiment have passed were of equal validity for the particular stage which human nature had reached ; and, though we may contrast, we may not judge these phases by the standards or canons of to-day. The fierce struggles of the early stage, instead of being condemned, are to be regarded as the necessary steps of an "eternal process moving on " by which adult opinion and sentiment have been reached ; just as the unlimited strife amongst the lower organisms in Nature has resulted in an elevation of the type, and in the survival of the fittest to live.

The advocates of empiricism and evolution, who have recently entered the lists as champions of their own position against the intuitional moralists, consistently affirm that there *is* no absolute standard of right and wrong: that it is the verdict of society — based on the unconscious perceptions of utility transmitted through a thousand generations — that makes a thing either right or wrong. Things are not to be done by us, because they are intrinsically right; they are right, because we do them ; that is to say, because *the race*, not the individual (who may be capricious), has agreed, through the consenting experience of centuries, to do them. Intuitional moralists, on the contrary, maintain that certain things are to be done, and others to be abstained from, in virtue of an intrinsic rightness or wrongness attaching to the acts themselves ; and that the assent of the race to a common rule (with manifold and inevitable exceptions, which both prove and illustrate it) is due, either to its progressive discernment of that intrinsic rightness, or to the unconscious sway of a principle of right reason which " worketh out of view," and which, though evolved by experience, is not its child.

Intuitional moralists affirm that the authority of the moral consciousness is weakened and degraded on every theory of evolution, *which is also a theory of derivation.* If the progressive experience of the race, refined, disciplined, and consolidated through many generations, has given rise to the moral faculty, the authority of that which has been thus derived is essentially affected by the disclosure of its genealogy. It is idle to allege that the discovery of its origin in mere sensation is not (as has been said) " to degrade the progeny, but to ennoble the ancestry ;" for if the honor of having produced a thing so totally unlike itself is conceded to sensation, the belief in its material origin may lessen the sanctity of virtue, while it suggests its commonplaceness. It may also chill the ardor with which virtue is pursued.

It is quite true that man may reverence that which he supposes to have sprung from the dust of the ground, as much as that which he imagines to have descended from the skies; but, dispensing with both these metaphoric modes of thought, we cannot reverence anything so devoid of character and coherence as a mere process of becoming, or stream of tendency, an endless genealogy without an original, a series of phenomena of which the only certain thing is that A is the antecedent of B, B of C, and so on *ad infinitum*. Moreover, in tracing the origin of the moral faculty by the light of evolution alone we cannot rest at mere sensation. We must go much farther back, and cannot pause consistently anywhere ; just as, in our anticipations of change in the future, we cannot rest at any conceivable goal, but must believe that a change in the moral *consensus* of the race will go on, till something totally unlike the present is reached. Both in our regress and in our progress, phenomena will be found which bear no resemblance to the present, but which nevertheless are, on the one hand, the elements out of which it has come, and on the other the product in which it must disappear. In this analysis of the moral sense we must go as far back and as far forward as we can; and when the torch of history fails us, and the paler light of archæology fades in the dimness of prehistoric surmise, the experience-philosophy tells us to step backwards into the darkness as trustfully as when we began our explanation of the facts of consciousness by its aid. We are not to stop at primitive man, or the primitive animal, but go back to the primitive protoplasm. The origin of the moral faculty must be sought beyond the twilight of sensation, in the blank midnight of the non-vital and purely physical forces. Conversely, we must suppose it not only possible but certain that in the millenniums of the future a wholly different product will be evolved out of the morals of our nineteenth century. We cannot draw a line, and say,

"Lo! *here*, across the line, the moral faculty is formed, is mature; whereas, *there*, on the other side of it, it was unformed and immature." It is always forming, maturing, changing; and it must undergo transformations into products as unlike the present, as these are unlike the contractile sensations of the ascidians in primeval seas. All things, according to the theory, are in perpetual motion; and the πόλεμος πάτερ πάντων of Heraclitus is as fully applicable to the paternity of the moral faculty as it is to the origin of the physical cosmos. In short, the universe tells us of the "ebb and flow," but not of the

> Ever-during Power,
> And central peace, subsisting at the heart
> Of endless agitation.

In opposition to the derivative theory of morals, the appeal of the intuitionalist is still, as it used to be in olden controversy, to the facts of consciousness; and, in the sphere of ethics, to the Absolute revealed in and disclosed to consciousness.

Students of the same problem, however, all appealing to consciousness, give us, as the result of that appeal, a different and opposite verdict. Like the rival sects with the same authoritative standard, the schools of Philosophy all turn to consciousness for their final testimony. And so,

> This is the book where each his dogma seeks,
> And this the book where each his dogma finds.

Nevertheless, we cannot dispense with the appeal. Consciousness is, and always must be, our final resort in every controversy. As we have no infallible arbiter, — and if we had one, his decisions would require the interpretation of consciousness, — all debate must end in, and all inquiry ultimately repose upon, the testimony of a disciplined reason, on enlightened consciousness. This interior light, directing without dictating, —and not the inductions of sense-perception, derived from objective phenomena, — is our only valid guide, and our sole arbiter in disputed problems.

> We perceive
> Within ourselves a measure and a rule,
> Which to the sun of truth we can apply,
> That shines for us, and shines for all mankind.

If we have evidence sufficient to warrant the conclusion that the phenomena of the moral consciousness are not explicable by evolution in the lifetime of the individual, our contention is, that evolution is incompetent to explain them, suppose you extend it to a million generations. If we cannot explain the origin of moral judgment by the principle of association in any single life, how should association be competent to explain its genesis for the race at large? If duty does not arise out of utility by the ascending steps of gradation in a single lifetime, why should a mere lengthening of the period enable it to do so? In the very limited field open to experimental research, we have no instance of the one passing into the other, or giving rise to it ; and we cannot concede that mere length of time will make amends for what the threescore years and ten of individual life, and the few thousand years of verifiable history, have failed to start.

If, within the range of human experience, we saw the process beginning — if we could trace the rudimentary signs of such a process at work, as the transformation of a sensation into a moral perception, or a discernment of utility into a conviction of duty, — we might by analogy suppose the process indefinitely extended, its area enlarged, and its significance enhanced. But the experimental fact, which should be the basis of the argument, is wanting. It is alleged that we have frequent instances of the love and pursuit of virtue, as a means to happiness, passing into a love and pursuit of it as an end, and for its own sake. But in none of the examples cited can we be sure that the love and pursuit belonged to these two separate categories in the respective stages. We do not know that there was not a love and pursuit of it for its own sake, though more dimly, at the first, and more explicitly afterwards; while considerations of utility may have been conjoined with this in both stages, at one time prominently, and again more faintly.

Many efforts have been made to trace the parentage of conscience to elements unlike itself. Mr. Maudsley tries to find its root in the most animal of all our instincts. More recently it has been said that the conviction of an inherent right to live is the germ out of which it has been evolved; a conviction which takes articulate shape in the proposition, " No one has a right to kill me," but which existed, in a rudimentary form, long before it expressed itself thus definitely.

If the conviction, " I have a right to live, no one has a right to kill me," be the germ out of which conscience has grown, we have first to account for the rise of that conviction itself, out of a state in which it was the normal law of the universe for the stronger to kill, and for the weaker to be killed. The whole difficulty is slurred over, if our explanation starts with a fully formed sense of personality, and the developed feeling of an inherent right to live. The problem to be solved is the reversal of the primitive rule of universal war, and indiscriminate struggle, when the only right was that of the strongest, and when no *individual* could have any right to live, because his strength was simply relative to the number and vigor of his competitors. The state supposed to be evolved out of this is a state in which, not only the stronger members of the race, but even the weakest individuals, come to feel that they have *an inherent right to live.* But can evolution, which is a mere process of becoming, explain this? Is it that, when the stronger have become proficient in the art of pushing their weaker comrades aside — when they have vanquished opposition and had a surfeit of slaughter—their sense of prowess gives rise to a new feeling that they have done well?   Do they, in virtue of their success in killing, win for themselves a right to survive?   Because of the number of their victims, do they purchase for themselves immunity from destruction? If so, —and it is difficult to see how otherwise it could be a case of evolution, pure and simple, —this is an instance of a principle evolved out of its own opposite! The hiatus between the stage in which it was natural that one animal should kill and that others should be killed, and the stage in which this became *un*natural, —and the conviction sprang up that each had a right to live and to continue in life, — is one that cannot be bridged over by any conceivable process of evolution, unless it be evolution by antagonism.   The one was a state in which our animal ancestors were wholly destitute of a sense of right, and could have no notion of a claim to live.

> For why? because the good old rule
> Sufficed them — the simple plan,
> That they should take who have the power,
> And they should keep who can.

The other is a state, not different from

this in degree, but diametrically opposite to it in kind, — a state in which each individual discerns the worth of his own personality, and his *inherent right* to exist.

If the chasm between these two stages is unbridged by evolution, does it fare any better with the next step in the process of development? Suppose that the persuasion, "I have a right to live," has been gradually manufactured out of its own opposite, how does the former give rise to the conviction that *another individual*, like me, has an equal right to live, and to live well? The prolonged life of the one was at first secured only by the constant death of competitors, in the struggle for existence. How did this give place to the conviction that the others — who might very possibly wish to kill the successful and surviving individual — had an equal right to live? No theory of evolution can answer this question, as no mere process of development can solve the problem of the genealogy of moral ideas.

Further, we have experimental proof, within the limits of our conscious life, that the Authority to which we bow is not derived from anything lower than itself. It carries the sign of its own absoluteness and non-contingency in the autocratic manner in which it announces itself. In the phenomena of conscience, we find the traces of a principle,

> Deep seated in our mystic frame,

not evolved out of the lower elements of appetency and desire, but controlling these, as an *alter ego*, "in us, yet not of us." Appearing at first simply as one amongst the other phenomena of consciousness, it mysteriously overshadows them; and suggests, in the occasional flashes of light sent across the darker background of moral experience, the working of a personality behind our own. As the seed quickens in the furrow when the surrounding elements coöperate to elicit its energy, so this latent faculty, awakening from its slumber during the process of moral education, is not the simple product of that process. The stimulus it receives merely liberates an imprisoned power. Thus liberated, it discerns its own original, not by retrospective glances along the narrow lines of individual or cosmological development; but, by a direct intuition of the reason, it gains

Fresh power to commune with the invisible world,
And hear the mighty stream of tendency
Uttering, for elevation of our thought,
A clear sonorous voice, inaudible
To the vast multitude.

ECLECTICISM.

I PROPOSE to discuss some of the features of Eclecticism, a philosophy which has received but scant justice from its critical successors.

It is both a system, and a tendency; a formal philosophical doctrine, and a spirit of philosophizing. At present it is not necessary to consider it historically, either in its strength or its weakness, as it appeared in the third century at Alexandria and Rome, at Athens in the fourth and fifth, or at Paris in the nineteenth; nor to deal with its secondary developments in social organizations, artistic schools, or religious systems. It is more important to ascertain its general speculative drift, its leading features, and permanent tendency. These may be seen, not only from the phases which it has assumed when formed into a coherent doctrine, but even more characteristically from its unconscious presence within the lines and under the limits of the systems which have ignored it. Wherever the effort to reconcile the claims of rival doctrines has taken the place of a one-sided advocacy of special views, the result, to the extent of the reconciliation, has been eclectic.

The term, however, is unfortunately misleading, as it seems to indicate the really elementary process of gathering together bits of systems, and arranging them in what must be at the best an artificial patchwork. No wonder that the result of a mere collection of *memorabilia*, however carefully made, should be a product without unity, coherence, or vitality. A system that resolved itself into a "golden treasury" of elegant extracts would deserve the neglect of all competent logicians, and of every serious thinker.[1]   And this is the ungenerous and inaccurate charge to which Eclecticism — the system suffering from

---

[1] On the same day on which this lecture was delivered, Dr. Martineau, in a profound and noble utterance from the Principal's Chair in Manchester New College, spoke of "an eclectic commonplace book of favorite beliefs" as "the last resort of superannuated philosophy." This remark will be appreciated perhaps most of all by those who carefully distinguish between "the commonplace book" and the system and spirit of Eclecticism.

its defective title — is sometimes exposed. It is difficult, however, to find a better word to describe it than this confessedly inaccurate and misleading one. The name of no system of philosophy is altogether adequate. The words "Idealist" and "Realist," "Ontologist" and "Experientialist," although convenient as indicating certain philosophical tendencies, are all inappropriate in some of their applications, and cannot be used with absolute rigor. The terms "Intuitionalism" and "Utilitarianism" are each misleading. The inadequacy of the word used to describe it is thus a misfortune which Eclecticism shares in common with every other system of opinion.

Keeping in view, therefore, what has already been said, viz., that its essential features exist in many systems which disown it, we shall find that the propositions which lie at the basis of Eclecticism are so self-evident, that in unfolding them we may seem to be stating a series of truisms. Out of their simplicity, however, profoundly important issues arise.

Eclecticism originates in the elementary but constantly forgotten fact that there is always truth on both sides of every great

controversy that has divided the thoughts
and feelings of mankind ; that error has
its origin — usually, if not always — in the
abuse of truth, in the exaggeration or travesty of fact ; that no intellectual doctrine
is absolutely and entirely false, or, root
and branch, a delusion ; that extravagance
in opinion usually proceeds from the ea-
gerness of devotees who carry true principles to false conclusions, and, in their
enthusiasm for a particular doctrine, forget its obverse. It is not that they are
wrong in the emphasis they throw on any
special truth, or group of truths. They
are only wrong in ignoring the fact that
each has a context dissimilar to itself,
though complementary and equally valid ;
and especially in forgetting that all major
truths are arranged in pairs, and may be
placed in the scales over against others of
equal weight and value ; so that, corresponding to every important doctrine, there
is always one equally great which bal-
ances it on the opposite side. When it
is said of rival systems that they are each
"resistless in assault, but impotent in defense," — although I would prefer to say,
resistless in defense while impotent in as-

sault, — what is meant is, that there is a citadel of strength (because a residuum of truth) at the heart of the most erroneous and extravagant, and that there is an element of weakness (because a tendency to bias or excess) associated with the truest that a progressive civilization has evolved. Thus the principle of Eclecticism contains a very obvious theory of the nature of truth and of error, and it offers an explanation of their origin respectively.

Let us suppose two minds, of different type or idiosyncracy, dealing with the same problem, — be it the origin of knowledge, or the conditions of responsibility, a doctrine of the beautiful, or a theory of conduct, — their hereditary intellectual tendencies vary, their temperaments are not the same, and their education has been different. They therefore approach the problem from opposite sides. Necessarily, they survey it in a different manner ; and their interpretation, however accurate, must be dissimilar. One will throw the stress on the subjective side of human knowledge, the other on the objective. The former, starting from the Ego, is idealistic throughout ; the latter, beginning with

Nature, is materialistic to the close. The one looks at man as a determined element in the material cosmos, and his ethical system is necessitarian; the other regards him as a free autonomous personality, and his system is libertarian. These different interpretations of the same problem, both true at the root, generate controversy. The differences increase; and schools of opinion arise, in which the opposite conclusions of the masters are intensified by their less original pupils. The chasm between them gradually widens; and, as the conflict grows, the partisans of each system retire to its strongholds, till the truth which each most loudly asserts is denied by its antagonist. The doctrines which were at the first accepted on both sides (on the one as major, and on the other as minor) become party badges, and in the end there is a fierce and sectarian denial of the opposing system. In intellectual and speculative theory, it is as in matters personal, social, and national. A minute divergence between two persons who are perhaps both in the right widens into a gigantic misunderstanding, or a slight diplomatic difference ripens into an international quarrel. And if, in most national quarrels, both nations are to blame, and in the majority of political party-contests neither side has a monopoly of justice, it is precisely so in the strife of the philosophical sects, in the controversies between artistic schools, and the warfare of religious parties.

Now suppose that the controversy between two philosophical sects has been protracted and keen. As with every other form of strife, the antagonism at length dies away, and, in the calmer and juster mood which succeeds, a desire springs up to reconcile, if possible, the opposite claims. A retrospective study of the controversy shows that the whole truth lay with neither party, that each had something real to defend, something worth defending, and that the strife between them was philosophically illegitimate; although, had there been no collision, the characteristic merits of each would not have been so prominently signalized. In the case of diametrically opposite theories, which negative each other, the excess of both is neutralized; and while each may establish the truth of its own affirmation, its negative or aggressive tendency is held in check by the mere presence of its opposite. Thus the antagonism of the schools preserves the philosophical world from the intolerant usurpation of any one of them, and brings out the special excellences of each.

A state of perpetual controversy amongst the sects, however, would do no particular good, if it did not lead to a better appreciation of their respective merits; and we find that an eclectic or reconciling movement generally follows, and is produced by, the controversies of the schools. It is gradually seen that each, if "right in what it affirmed," was "wrong in what it denied;" right in so far as it was positive, and wrong only in its negation of the *locus standi* or *jus vivendi* of the systems it sought to annihilate.[1]

---

[1] It is to Leibnitz that we owe the phrases I have quoted in the text, and there is perhaps no name in the roll of modern philosophy whose appreciation of the spirit and aim of Eclecticism was more thorough than his. "I have tried," he says, "to disinter, and to reunite the truth, buried and dissipated under the opinions of the sects of the philosophers." (*Trois lettres* à *M. Remond de Montmort*, Opera, ed. Erdmann, p. 701.) "I have found that most of the sects are right in a large part of what they affirm, but not in what they deny.

The human mind cannot find repose either in the onesidedness of a partisan system, or in the absolute repression of partisanship, and the substitution in its plan of such eclecticism as shrinks from the expression of difference. The eclecticism I am expounding is assuredly not one which would adjust differences, and end controversy, by the adoption of mild and

. . . I flatter myself that I have penetrated to the harmony of the several realms of philosophy " (he is speaking of the materialists and the idealists), " and have seen *that both parties are in the right, if only they would not exclude each other* " (p. 702). Again (letter iii. p. 704), " Truth is often wider spread than one thinks; but it is very often overlaid, and very often covered up ; and weakened, mutilated, and corrupted by additions which spoil it, or render it less useful. In getting hold of the traces of Truth amongst the Ancients, or, to speak more generally, our predecessors, one must draw gold out of mud, the diamond from the mine, and light from darkness. Thus would we reach the *philosophia perennis.*" So too Cousin, " There is no absolutely false system, but many incomplete ones, systems true in themselves, but erroneous in their pretense each to comprehend within itself that absolute truth which is only to be found in them all. The incomplete, and therefore the exclusive, that is the one radical vice of Philosophy, or rather of the philosophers, because philosophy is in all the systems. Each system is a reflection of reality, but unfortunately it reflects it only under a single angle." (*Fragmens Philosophiques*, i. p. 242, " Du Fait de Conscience.")

hazy commonplaces, which no sect or
school could possibly deny. It conserves
every intellectual difference that is the
outcome of distinctive thought, and of a
true interpretation of the universe; only,
it makes room, alongside of each interpretation, for others that have usually been
held to be inconsistent and incompatible
with it.

But, as it is in the union of one or two
historical facts, with sundry psychological
phenomena, that Eclecticism may be said
to find its stronghold, I pass to the consideration of these.

In the first place, there is the historical fact of the incessant rise of new systems, their inevitable decay, and their perpetual reappearance. Why do systems of
opinion pass away from the thought and
the allegiance of mankind, but from the
radical imperfection which necessarily char-
acterizes them; from their adequacy for
a time, their inadequacy for all time?
Why do they reappear again, but from the
root of truth which they contain? The
mere fact of the resurrection of old and
apparently exploded doctrines is a historic
proof of their superiority to the assault

that seemed to lay them low. It shows
that the conflict of opinion — however interesting as mental gladiatorship, and however valuable as a means of developing
knowledge, and sifting truth from error —
is a conflict which in the end leaves no one
absolute master of the field. If the controversy is renewed, if the strife begins
again, it is because the forces on neither
side were silenced, and because each is
able to return to the combat with unex-
hausted courage and fresh resource.

The next fact is the impossibility (judg-
ing by analogy) of uniformity of belief,
and therefore of the cessation of controversy ever occurring in the history of the
world, — a consummation which is probably no more possible, and no more desirable, than the cessation of physical storms,
and the substitution of perpetual calm and
sunshine. This, — the necessity of fresh
controversy, — though generally recognized
as a feature in the progress of civilization,
has perhaps never been adequately appraised, and its corollaries have certainly
not been always seen. It involves the
certainty of the rise of new types of philosophical thought and belief, while the

human race continues to advance. With every new cycle will come a new phase of insight, and a new attitude of feeling towards the universe. Does any one, except the merest tyro in historical knowledge, or the most youthful champion of debate, expect the advent of a time when speculative controversy will cease, and the opposition of the schools disappear? Such a result would imply either a radical alteration in the structure of human nature, or the extinction of belief in an ideal, and the collapse of effort to reach it. It would be the very dullest and dreariest world in which every man agreed with every other man upon every conceivable topic. It would imply the decadence of the intellect, the withering of the imagination, and the stoppage of the pulse of the human heart. It would amount, in short, to an arrest laid on the mainsprings of civilization. And where are we to draw the line between an agreement on every possible problem, and a general concurrence in the greater problems, as finally solved for the human race? Is not the distinction only one of degree? If absolute uniformity of opinion is impossible, is general concurrence less utopian?

But *why* must systems of opinion run through their cycles, and reappear? Why are the intellectual differences, which culminate in opposing doctrines, destined to remain as permanent and indelible tendencies of human nature? Are there any psychological facts which explain how they have hitherto existed, and justify the inference that they will continue to characterize the future evolution of humanity.

One explanation is, that every developed opinion, no matter how contorted and extravagant it may be, has sprung from some real root in the soil of human nature. It has been evolved; and if evolved, its formative principle cannot have been mere vagary, hap-hazard, or blind caprice. Grant that it was often a crude guess, a surmise, a thought casually thrown out at an object, that gave rise to primitive belief. These guesses were the offspring of previous intelligence, and the precursors of genuine knowledge. The surmises, which grew out of vague unillumined gropings, were disciplined by degrees into real insight, definite and verifiable. But each separate surmise, of necessity, directed towards a particular aspect of Nature or of

Life, was different from the rest; and the result of the difference is seen in the various "doctrines of knowledge" and "systems of the universe," or "theories of existence," which now divide or distract the world. The source of the difference has been chiefly within the individual theorist. It has been due to temperament, and hereditary tendency, although also, in a minor degree, to the education and surroundings of the system builder.

Given a certain temperament, ancestry, education, and influence, it is quite possible to predict the system that will naturally emerge; to say whether it will be intuitional or experiential, idealist or realist, *a priori* or *a posteriori*. Up to one half of the result, it is altogether beyond the individual's control, and is as rigidly determined for him as is the color of his hair, or the height of his stature, his nationality, or his mode of speech. Diversity will therefore necessarily characterize all future systems of opinion and belief. This diversity will be due to the immense variety of the forces that sway human nature, which is a fact of equal magnitude and significance with its underlying

unity, — a variety which is not only consistent with the unity, but which illustrates it, and goes on developing alongside
of it. It may thus be said that on the one
hand the unity of human nature, and on
the other its variety, constitute the root
and ground of eclecticism. If the race is
one in organic structure, in mental endow-
ment, in moral tendency, in imaginative capacity, and in spiritual possibility, — despite
the thousand varieties which proclaim our
separateness and individuality, — the outcome of this unity, in the endless systems
we construct for the explanation of the
abiding mystery of the universe, must in
every instance possess a greater or less
degree of truth. On the other hand, the
variety which marks us off from one
another, the differences which separate us
— despite our organic unity and the solidarity of the race — must of necessity give
rise to fresh forms of dogma and belief.
Our speculative doctrines being sifted and
refined by controversy, our frames of theory
will correspond more and more adequately
to the truth of things, while they differ
from the older ones, which they supersede.
We may thus expect a simultaneous de-

velopment and deepening, both of the unity
and the variety of human nature, its diversity in opinion, feeling, and practice, its
unity in aspiration and aim.

Here I may put a question, which, however simple, deserves consideration. What
is the meaning of the belief that two antagonist systems can be reconciled, and of
the attempts made to effect the reconciliation? — for example, that the philosophy
of experience can be reconciled with that
of intuition, or even that the claims of Religion and Science can be adjusted? that
there is no necessary collision in the nature
of things between the two, but only between
sundry mistaken versions or interpretations of each? If the experiential and the
a priori systems of knowledge can be har-
monized, if the intuitional and the derivative theories of morals can be reconciled,
it is because every system of the universe
that has been evolved from the brain of
man must have arisen from some germ of
reality, and because its error has been
simply a distortion of the truth.

Add to this, that every published system of opinion — or that portion of it
which can be epitomized and exhibited in

a reasoned treatise — is only a small portion of it. A large context is never exhibited to view; and just as a man may
be intellectually refuted without being
convinced, because what has been refuted
is only that portion of his opinions which
was revealed and expressed in words, — the
context, lying within his mind undivulged,
being also untouched by argument, — so
the vital part of every dogma may be a
subterranean element, a root unconscious
to the individual, and never exposed to
view. If its upper growth is cut down,
like those perennial plants of which while
the stem decays the root survives, it will
send forth flowers next season freshly as
before.

We may thus see how action and reaction is an inevitable and abiding feature in
human opinion and belief; how the truth
and the error of "systems" is but a question of degree; how their vitality is due
to the truth they contain, and their longevity to the amount of that truth; how
immortality, in the sense of abiding continuity, is the prerogative of none; while
resurrection and rehabilitation may be the
destiny of each. It is impossible for an

individual, or a generation, to have an equally clear grasp, and an equally firm hold, of the opposite and balancing sides of any truth ; and the prominence, which the individual or the age may give to any special view, always leads by reaction to a corresponding predominance, in the next age, of some other view. So soon as any truth is generally recognized, and its novelty has passed away, it falls by a natural process into the background of the human consciousness. Another truth, which could not get full justice during the ascendency of the former, is brought to light, is disinterred if not discovered ; and its advocacy has the charm of novelty for a time, till it too shares the fate of its predecessor, and sinks into the shade, to make room for its perishable successor. But this is not the mere rise and fall of systems, and their reappearance, precisely as they lived before. Nothing ever wholly dies ; but nothing returns to visible life under the old form. It is changed, both by its previous existence in the field of human consciousness, and by its temporary absence from it, by its departure and its return.

Besides, as every dominant doctrine tends

at once and insensibly to become sectarian, the best antidote to the evil of one-sidedness is usually a counter movement towards the other side, even although it be a movement in excess across the dividing line. Thus the error of idealism is met by materialistic reaction, and *vice versa.* The evils of extreme necessitarianism are counteracted by an extreme doctrine of liberty. The enthusiastic advocacy of a truth long disesteemed is not only sure to provoke hostility, but its excess is most easily counterworked from a position on the other side of the golden mean. Enthusiasm for a particular truth is always beautiful, and often useful ; but, as its advocate may become its idolater, the bias of his enthusiasm is best restrained by a counter enthusiasm for some other truth. The exaggeration is inevitable, and is excellent while it lasts. It becomes pernicious only if it lasts too long.

The student of the history of Philosophy may at first be perplexed by the number of opposing systems, and by the curious hostilities of the system-builders. But so soon as he turns from the field of history to investigate the human consciousness,

and discovers the number of conflicting
elements that are there, he ceases to wonder at the diversities of the schools. The
latter are but a sign of the fertility, the
resource, and the wealth of human nature.

The disparagement of the labors of predecessors, however, — which is a failing of
so many philosophers — may surprise and
disappoint the student of their works ;
more especially if he observes how much
they have been indebted to their predecessors, if not for hints which they have expanded, at least for the direction which
their labors have taken.

The explanation is easy. The ability to
do justice to past systems of opinion is a
rare intellectual quality, especially if it be
combined with original genius and actual
discovery. The ambition of founding or
completing a system disinclines the mind
to admit the humbling fact that very much
of what seems original has been already
said, in another form, and that there is ex-
ceedingly little that is new under the sun.

The illusion of originality, nevertheless,
has its uses. Most minds are urged to un-
dertake research by the prospect of original
discovery. Were the reappearance of an

old system, in a new dress or dialect, to be
surmised beforehand, one stimulus to continued speculative labor would be removed.
In other words, it is the illusion of originality that is the chief spur to philosophical
activity.

The misrepresentation of former systems, to which I have alluded, itself explains the rise of new ones. Misconception of the nature or tendency of any
doctrine usually provokes a reaction in its
favor, and originates a desire to do it justice ; and so the old opinion returns in a
new form. It is true of systems as of
individuals : they must be misconstrued,
before they develop their finest characteristics. They take deeper root, in the
storm of adverse criticism. If all men
spoke well of a speculative doctrine, it
would be as injurious to its development,
as universal praise would be hurtful to the
character of its founder.

It is to be further noted that many
philosophical systems differ in appearance
more than in reality. Their antagonism
is on the surface ; deeper down they unite.
The difference may, as I have remarked,
be simply one of emphasis. at the particu-

lar point where the stress of the system is laid.   This fact is so important that it may be restated thus.   Two systems, let us say, start from the same first principle.   There they are at one.   But the agreement is hidden, is subterranean.   They proceed to develop what they hold in common.   What seems major to one is minor to another, and *vice versa*.   This sense of difference, intensified by every fresh glance towards the first principle, by slow degrees widens the breach.   The emphasis repeated — like the slow modifications of organic structure, of which science has told us so much, and by which it has explained so much — results in the formation of a new opinion.

If any one wishes to realize the latter process, let him first study the law of natural selection and the survival of the fittest, in physical nature.   Then if he wants to find that law confirmed, let him watch, by the light of history, the evolution of human opinion.   Only let the stress continue to be laid on one side of a truth, which has two sides, both equally important ; what is thus emphasized will beget a new type of opinion, which may grow into a product so unlike that from which it sprung, that the parentage and the derivation are scarcely recognizable. But the result will have been wholly due to an increase of emphasis, thrown entirely on one side.

It follows from this that the most distinctive feature in each of the philosophical schools is admitted — in some form or other — by all the rest ; only it is *subordinated* to other features which have the front place of honor. We may have to search for it in what I may call the crypts, or underground recesses of the system ; but, if we do so, we will find — it may be concealed, or it may be almost obliterated — the very truth which forms the centre-point of the rival philosophical school. For example, Socrates and the Sophists held much in common, and their original conflict was due to the importance which the former attached to truths which the latter only subordinated. The same is seen still more significantly in the conflict between the Stoics and the Epicureans, and preëminently in the great ethical controversy of the ages as to Freedom and Necessity.

Thus when we criticise a particular system, and say, " What So-and-so holds in

A — referring to one part of his doctrine — cannot be reconciled with what he holds in B — referring to another part of it, — his system is inconsistent," what does the criticism mean but that he has taken more facts into account than his system can rationally explain, or than he can make coherent? In other words, it amounts to this: that the man is larger than his system, his humanity is wider than his interpretation of human nature.

It has been said, however, that whenever Eclecticism ceases to be a mere spirit of philosophizing, and becomes a system of philosophy, it is false to its own first principle. In the very act of laying the foundations of a school, the eclectic, it is said, becomes a sectarian, and commits an act of intellectual suicide. It is therefore affirmed that Eclecticism should be a regulative principle in all systems, and the outcome of all, without being the distinctive badge of any one; that it should be a tendency rather than a school, a way of looking at systems of opinion, that is sympathetic, fair-minded, and friendly, rather than antagonistic and critical. We must consider this objection.

That it should be a prevailing spirit in all philosophy, and that it cannot crystallize into a dogma without belying its own principles, is undoubted. Further, if it exists as a tendency or attitude, although ignored as a system, it is practically of the greatest value. Hence its immense importance to the student of history. It supplies him with a double key, explanatory at once of the philosophy of History, and the history of Philosophy. But if, while the spirit of eclecticism guides the constructive labor of the system-builder, he still keeps to the groove of his system, and declines to assume the *rôle* of the eclectic, he remains sectarian. Either one of two things must result: he must keep to his system as a distinctive party badge, and disown what he will doubtless consider the vague position of the eclectic; or his eclecticism must conquer his system.

The intellectual quality of fair-mindedness has a front place in the hierarchy of the virtues; but it may exist as a tendency, without penetrating to the very core of the constructive reason, and moulding the system that results. The highest merit of eclecticism is its doing full justice to the systems that partially understand, yet formally repudiate it. As it is the supreme triumph of charity to include the uncharitable within the area it traverses, — to see something good even in the intolerance that is persecuting, and that would if possible extinguish what it cannot comprehend, — so, it is the crowning excellence of the eclectic spirit that it sees some latent good in the most *outré* and distorted system that has ever disfigured the annals of civilization.

But in its effort to do justice to every other doctrine, it has not always been just to itself. It has sometimes become a martyr to its own generosity. Hence it has been stigmatized as too mild and diffusive, as the glorification of a weak live-and-let-live system. Many of those who esteem its tendency, despise it as a formulated theory ; and while the speculative world refuses permanently to adopt any sectarian theory of knowledge or of life, it has never cordially welcomed the eclectics. It has shown a greater repugnance to acquiesce in this doctrine as the last word of Philosophy, than to adopt those sectarian extremes, which Eclect-

icism tries to unite and reconcile. How
is this? Can it be explained? Yes; the
eclectic can explain it.

There can be no doubt that, in proportion to the width and elasticity of a system, is its want of fitness as a working
theory of knowledge and life — as a doctrine that can be applied to human affairs.
So true is the maxim of Goethe, "Thought
widens, but lames; action narrows, but
animates." This is owing to the fact that
all activity is, and must be, carried on in
grooves. If we are to work in a world of
limitations, we must submit to our limits,
and not chafe under them. We may sit
apart,

> Holding no form of creed,
> But contemplating all;

but when we do so, we retire from our
place and our duties, in a world of imperfect action, and of necessarily incomplete
fulfillment.

Constituted as we are, it is impossible
for our intellectual vision, however wide
the horizon it may sweep, to take in more
than a very few and limited group of
objects at any one time. What results
from this? It is the temporary promi-

nence of one truth or fact or law, or of one group of truths, facts, and laws, which strike the eye of the beholder, arrest his attention, and rouse him to action. If he saw the other and bordering truths which balance the ones he sees, mitigating their force and regulating their sway, — truths which other eyes are seeing while his do not, — he could scarcely be roused to the defense or the upholding of the former ones. His enthusiasm would certainly cool, and his energy might collapse. Does any one imagine that if the child had, in his childhood, a presage of the wisdom of the man, he would show any ardor in the pursuit of those "childish things" which age sees to be illusory? If then the experientialist, the utilitarian, the ontologist, the idealist, were more eclectic than they usually are, if they saw the full merit of the systems they oppose, — while their denunciations would be less loud, and their antagonism less pronounced, — inaction, and perhaps indifference, might take the place of energy. It is not difficult to see why catholicity often leads to inaction, why toleration and supineness go hand in hand; and why,

with the narrower vision of the sectarian
thinker, is usually associated the propa-
gandist ardor of the partisan.

From this we may deduce a corollary.
In criticising extremes of opinion, which
in their ultra forms are to be condemned,
the main point is to recognize the mean,
and intellectually to return to it, for the
preservation of intellectual harmony ; but
to understand departure from it, not merely
for the sake of practical action, but for the
comprehension of the mean itself. Every
time we act, we depart from the mean, for
the mean state is one of torpor and repose.
Since, however, we must act, in one way or
another, we must also cross the medial line
between extremes, even while we do not
lose sight of it, or permit the intellectual
eye to be closed to it. If, as already remarked, monotony would characterize the
beliefs of mankind, were all the members of
the human race to see eye to eye, the dreariest results would follow if all men equally
shunned the "falsehood of extremes ;" because *it is the extremes that make the mean
intelligible.* Thus, the seemingly illogical
position is reached : there is an advantage
to the human race in its partial glimpses

of truth, in its temporary, if it be not
a stationary, one-sidedness in thought and
action.

Here I must allude to a doctrine of Jouffroy, the distinguished successor of Cousin
in the French eclectic school. He says
that as truth and error are mixed in every
system, if truth be one and error various,
the variety of the systems is due to their
departures from truth ; and he even affirms
that the succession of the schools is owing
to the error they contain, each being a
fugitive mirror of an out-reaching reality.
I do not think that systems of opinion differ only in the erroneous elements they
include. I would rather say that the distinctive badge of each is the particular
truth which it is its merit to have signalized, and made emphatic. The wise man
searching for truth finds its fragments
everywhere, its entire presence nowhere.
In every system he sees it partial, dismem-
bered, isolated ; hence he is both a believer
in evolution, and necessarily a student of
history.

Eclecticism and development go hand
in hand. No consistent evolutionist can
be other than eclectic. All systems hav-

ing, according to his theory, been evolved out of antecedent ones, — and it being his function to trace the lineage and genealogy of each, — all have an equal claim to be regarded with honor. Nay more, every link in the chain of derivation, being a necessary sequence, is worthy of equal intellectual respect,— a respect quite inconsistent with the railing of some evolutionists against certain products that have been evolved. According to their theory, as the glacier shapes the valley and the sea its beach, ancestral tendencies and uncontrollable contemporary forces shape the beliefs of the untoward generation that refuses to accept their doctrines. And why should they be more irritated at the philosophy or religion that surrounds them, than at the denudation of the valley, or the raising of the sea-beach?

We are sometimes met, however, with the charge that Eclecticism and Skepticism go hand in hand. A consideration of this will lead both to a final vindication of the claims of Philosophy, and to a further explanation of the rise and fall of "systems" of opinion. The two propositions, that no system is final, and that none is exhaustive, carry with them the fundamental postulate of eclecticism ; but this does not give to every system an equal rank, or an equivalent value as a theoretical embodiment of the truth of things. It is true that if I call no philosopher "master," it is because *all* are masters within their respective spheres, and because other masters will yet arise to teach the generations of the future; while the sphere of truth itself outreaches every possible chart which any of them may construct. Any one system of the universe, however, is truer than another, not in proportion to the number of the elements it embraces, but in proportion to the accuracy with which it interprets the elements with which it deals.

One advantage of a wise and sympathetic study of the history of opinion is, that it enables us to dispose satisfactorily of a charge often ignorantly brought against the claims of Philosophy. The charge is that it is a barren study, yielding no results which are demonstrably certain, and can be taken for granted in the investigations of the future. The march of the physical sciences is pointed to as one of consecutive conquest and progressive discovery, with no circular movements, or serpentine windings, or dubious returnings on former tracks. Even brilliant "histories of philosophy" have been written with the aim of proving that Philosophy is an illusion. Its course is represented as a series of voyages by bold adventurers on the illimitable waters, without ever touching, or even seeing, the "happy isles," and with many experiences of shipwreck and disaster.

In support of this, we are pointed to the rise and fall of systems; and we are asked either to select one out of the conflicting multitude, and prove it to be orthodox, or to abandon the study of Philosophy as resultless.

The only satisfactory way of dealing with this objection is to get at the cause of the rise and fall of all the systems that have ever existed in the schools, or in the world outside the schools. If we clearly apprehend, not only the reason why this or that opinion has happened to prevail at a particular time, but the source or origin of all systems, actual or possible, the reasonableness and the value of philosophical study

will be self-evident. It will be seen to be,
on the one hand, the study of the natural
history of the human mind; and, on the
other, the study of the very problem with
which the human faculties have been incessantly occupied. Every speculative system is a memorial of the effort made by
man to interpret that mysterious Text
which the universe presents to his faculties for interpretation. It is an attempt
to explain the ultimate meaning of the
things that environ us in the world without, and occur in the world within. Every
system that has ever appeared is thus *a
theory of the meaning of Existence;* and is
therefore a partial unfolding of the onward
thought of humanity, directed to this problem. We may safely hazard the assertion
that there must be some truth in *all* of
these systems, if there is truth in *any one* of
them. However defective it may be, each
is a landmark or index of progress. It has
not only contributed to the development of
the world's thought, it has been a necessary *part* of it.

And, for the same reason, it becomes
superannuated and passes away. No system can expand beyond a certain limit;

but, while it ceases to flourish — and seems to pass away — what really happens is this. The development of human intellect and insight, which has been going on for a time in one direction, pauses *in that direction*, and begins to unfold itself along another line. It progresses by alternate ebb and flow, or by alternate beats of action and reaction. No "system" — philosophical, religious, artistic, or social — can, in the nature of things, go on expanding forever; any more than a tree, or a flower, can expand forever. But the human mind continues to expand, the organic thought of the world develops, the flowering of the general consciousness goes on; and all the systems, which record and register these, are merely historical memorials, by which the rise of intellect and feeling, in certain directions, and to a particular height, is marked. Thus the hope of attaining a finally perfect, or absolutely orthodox philosophy — a "system" that shall compose the controversies of the ages, and end the strife of rival schools — is utopian. It is the fond illusion of speculative youth, which passes away in the more sober judgments of experience, especially if these

judgments are formed under the light of
history. And it disappears, not because
truth is despaired of, or because so little of
it can be known, but because so much of
it is seen, and is seen scattered everywhere
in fragments.

If therefore the history of Philosophy
shows the incessant swing of the pendulum of thought between opposite poles of
opinion, if destructive systems are followed
by constructive ones, if the skeptic succeeds the dogmatist, if an idealistic reaction follows in the wake of every materialistic movement, the explanation is easy.
It is not only that one extreme invariably
gives rise to its opposite, and that the two
act and react upon each other ; it is also
that both are always present, within humanity itself. It is constantly forgotten
that our "systems of opinion" are only an
illustration of certain permanent tendencies
of human nature. They exhibit the upper
or surface sign of an underworking current,
which is ceaselessly moving on, often quite
unknown to the system-makers, — like those
vast tidal waves, of the rise and fall of which
the voyager on the Atlantic is wholly unconscious. The reason why one and an-

other "system" is dominant, and the reason why they all reappear (after falling for a time into the shade), is that they represent ineradicable phases of thought, and are, therefore uneliminable elements in human civilization. It is thus that the doctrines of the world's youth reappear in its age that the systems of ancient India are seen in modern Germany, and that the thought of the old Greek sages has a resurrection in Oxford and Berlin. If any symbol is permissible in Philosophy it is that of the phœnix.

Perhaps the most signal service which eclecticism has rendered to the cause of human progress is the new way of looking at History, and the historical schools, which it has introduced. A wide knowledge of the history of opinion has often given rise to catholicity in philosophical theory ; and although all historians have their bias, no study is more helpful to width of view, or is more emphatically the parent of fair-mindedness. But the benefit is reciprocal. If historical study promotes Eclecticism, by showing that its basis is broadly laid in the region of fact and event, the eclectic spirit is one of the best safeguards to the historian. It preserves him from the taint of partisanship. It animates the study of the driest details with living interest, by connecting them with their causes and their issues. It has done immense service to human progress by showing that the true function of the historical critic is not so much to expose illusions, as to ascertain their origin ; to rise above, by getting behind them ; and to discover the living root whence error has sprung, and of which it is the distortion. It is thus opposed to every form of iconoclasm. In so far as our liberal teachers and thinkers are iconoclasts, in so far as they are irreverent towards the past or towards the present, they are non-eclectic, sectarian, revolutionary ; and the practical merit of the system I have been trying to expound — a merit probably greater than the most perfect theoretical consistency would be — is its large tolerance, its spirit of conciliation rather than of compromise, and its detection of truth underneath all the exaggeration, distortion, and caricature of the systems that have from time to time emerged.

PERSONALITY AND THE INFI-NITE.

It is one of the most noticeable facts in the history of opinion that speculative doctrines, which become sharply antagonistic when carried to their legitimate results, are found to harmonize at the basis whence they spring. There, they may even touch each other, while their developed conclusions may be as wide as the poles asunder. It has been said that opposite errors have usually a common πρῶτον ψεῦδος. It is perhaps truer to affirm that all antagonistic theories take their rise from an underlying root of truth. The history of philosophy shows how easily differences, which are trivial at their first appearance, develop into distinctive schools of opinion, and how rapidly they are confirmed by the reaction and antagonism of rival systems.

The question whether the supreme Being, or ultimate Existence within the universe, is in any sense personal, — whether it can be legitimately spoken of, and interpreted by us, in the terms in which we speak of, and interpret our own personality, is as old as the discussions of the Eleatics in Greece; and from Parmenides to Hegel it has been solved in one way, while from the Jewish monotheists, through the entire course of Christian theology, it has been answered in another. National temperament and racial tendency have had their influence in determining the character of these answers; and we may perhaps affirm that the instinct of the Semitic races has tended in one direction, while that of the Aryan, or Indo-European, has tended in another. If recent discussion of the subject in contemporary literature contributes little to the solution of this controversy of the ages, it has the merit of presenting the perennial problem in a singularly clear light; and it proves how the most abstruse questions of human knowledge continue to fascinate the heart, and to tax the intellect of man, while they directly affect his practical life.

The late David Frederick Strauss, and the brilliant literary critic — Matthew Arnold — have each written strongly against the notion of personality in God; the former, consistently developing the Hegelian doctrine, which he has applied to the problems of religious history; the latter, endeavoring to lay the basis of a new reverence for the Bible, through a phenomenal psychology and doctrine of ignorance, in those delightful, though confessedly unsystematic papers in the Contemporary Review,[1] full of delicate and happy criticism, though dashed too much with *persiflage*, and scarcely grave enough when the radical importance of the question is considered, in connection with the literature of solemn speculation on the subject.

Mr. Arnold has been telling us that we must give up and renounce forever the delusion that God is "a person who thinks and loves." We are to recognize instead "a stream of tendency, by which all things fulfill the law of their being;" a "power that lives and breathes and feels," but not "a person who thinks and loves." We are directed, as all the world knows, to "the eternal not-ourselves that makes for righteousness." But does this curious entity, this "eternal not-ourselves," present a more

---

[1] Afterwards published in his book, *God and the Bible.*

adequate notion to the intellect than that which it is meant to displace? Is it less ambiguous, or less hypothetical? We are asked to substitute, for the exploded notion of a personal God, a negative entity of which all that can with certainty be affirmed is that it is "not we ourselves," that it is beyond us and eternal. All else is to be set aside as personification and poetry, or "extra-belief." But would not an "eternal-in-ourselves" making for righteousness be a more intelligible, an equally relevant, and equally verifiable notion? And how do we know it to be "eternal," but by an *a priori* process, which the new philosophy would disown? and is "a power that feels" more intelligible, or verifiable, than "a power that thinks?" We are supposed to be conducted, by the help of this definition, out of the dim regions of theological haze, to the *terra firma* of verifiable knowledge. Is it then less intricate and confusing than the old historic conception, which it is intended to supplant? No one, it is said, "has discovered the nature of God to be personal, or is entitled to assert that God *has* conscious intelligence." But we are told to look to "the constitution and history of things," where we find an "eternal tendency" at work "outside of us, prevailing whether we will or no, whether we are here or not;" and we shall find that this eternal *non-ego* "makes for righteousness."

The special merit which the new definition claims for itself is that it is a luminous one, and that it is within the range of experience, where it can be tested and verified. Now, in this demand for verification, Mr. Arnold either wishes our religious philosophy to be recast in terms of the exact sciences, and nothing accepted in the sphere of psychology and metaphysic which cannot be reached as we reach conclusions in mathematics; or he is stating a philosophical commonplace, viz., that moral truth is not susceptible of demonstrative evidence. Are not the terms he makes use of, however, both loose and deceptive? This "making for righteousness" is meant to describe the action of a vast impersonal tendency, everywhere operative towards that end. But surely all our experience of "tendency" in the direction of righteousness is personal. Observation of the results of human action, of the consequences of wrong-doing and of righteous conduct respectively, shows that certain causes, set in motion by ourselves or by others, issue in certain subjective effects. If we confine ourselves to the sphere of experience, we not only get no farther than the observation of phenomena, but all the succession we observe is personal, because it is the field of human conduct alone that is before us. In thus limiting ourselves, however, another fact arrests our notice. If there be a stream of tendency, not ourselves, that makes for righteousness, there is also a stream of tendency, not ourselves, that makes for wickedness. There are *two* streams of tendency flowing through the universe, into one or other of which all the lesser rills of influence flow. We can trace their fluctuating course, from the early centuries to the present time; but what the better are we of either, as a solution of the ultimate problem of the universe? If we confine ourselves to the limited area open to inductive inference, and the verifications of experience, we cannot reach the conclusion that there is a single stream of tendency, not ourselves and beneficent, which makes for righteousness alone. If certain phenomena seem to warrant this inference, counter-appearances suggest, with equal force, the operation of a malignant power, making persistently for evil ; and with two antagonistic forces in perpetual collision, the conditions of ditheism are complete, and the Manichean doctrine is reached.

Returning to the formula against which Mr. Arnold has directed so many shafts of criticism, viz., that God is "a person who thinks and loves," I have no hesitation in accepting it as a substantially accurate definition of what is held by the majority of theists ; although, perhaps few would state it in these terms, and it is liable to misconception, chiefly through the use of the indefinite article. If Mr. Arnold were merely cautioning us against identifying our notion of what constitutes personality in God, with our concept of personality in man, — if his teaching on this point were but a warning against the popular tendency to assume, either that human nature was an adequate measure of the Divine, or that it afforded our only light as to the characteristics of the Divine, — it would be most salutary ; although it would be merely a continuation of the familiar mes-

sage of the seers of Israel, a modern
echo of the prophetic voices of the Hebrew Church, when they affirmed that He
is "not altogether such an one as ourselves." It amounts, however, to much
more than this. It is an echo of the
dogma which lies at the heart of every
monistic system of speculation ; viz., that
there is a radical inconsistency, or contradiction, between the notions of the Personal and the Infinite, so that we cannot
combine both in a concept which conserves the characteristics of each ; but
must, in logical consistency, surrender the
one, or the other ; that, in short, if God be
a person, He cannot be infinite ; and if infinite, He must be impersonal. Personality is regarded as, in all cases, essentially
limited, and necessarily bounded. In the
human race, the personality of each man
is supposed to consist in his isolation from
his fellows ; and it is inferred that all personality consists in a gathering together of
self, at a centre or focus of individuality ;
that it is realizable and real, only in its
separation from, and exclusion of, other
things ; while it is affirmed that the Absolute and Infinite are all-embracing and all-

surrounding, excluding nothing, but enfolding within themselves the totality of existence. Therefore, it is said, if there be an infinite and absolute Being in the universe, nothing else can exist besides. He will take up and include within himself all existence whatsoever; but, in so doing, he cannot be personal; for the personal is always the bounded, the fenced, the separate, the inclosed.

To put the difficulty which the theistic solution presents in its strongest light, I restate the problem thus: Endeavoring to realize the infinite, whether in space or in time, we may begin by imagining circles beyond circles, or lines of continuous succession unbroken by any point or interval. We rise on the wings of imagination, and pursue the journey till thought sinks paralyzed. But in so doing, we have never really got one step beyond the finite. By such imaginative flights along the lines of sequence, or over areas of space, we never approach one whit nearer to the Infinite; and why? because the vastest conceivable aggregate of finites is not really liker it, than is the unit from which we start, in the process of multiplication.

The one is but the other "writ large."
Therefore, we may not only reach the notion as well before the journey of finite
thought commences, but if we reach it at
all, it must be by a process wholly different from an expansion of the finite, and by
the exercise of another faculty than that of
imagination.

We may reach it, however, in a moment, not by a multiplication of the finite,
but by its elimination ; not by enlarging
the notion, but by abolishing it. All conceivable finites being before the mind, as
an indefinite quantity, we may say with
Herder, "These I remove, and thou — the
Infinite — liest all before me." Our
speculative thought of the Infinite is not
a pictorial or concrete realization of it as
a mental image, built up out of elements
furnished by sense-experience, or imaginatively bodied forth on the inner horizon
of the mind. We do not reach it by a
synthetic process, piecing together a multitude of finite things, sweeping round
them, and imagining them in their totality.
But we at once and directly think away
all limitation, and abolish the finite, by
excluding individual determinate things,

from a field preoccupied by thought. Now, with this idea of the Infinite — as the negation of the finite — is it possible to conjoin the notion of anything whatever that is personal? Personality manifests itself to us familiarly, under the restrictions of finite form. It is difficult to conjoin it even with the notion of the indefinitely vast. As you approach the latter, the former seems to recede. Is there an intellectual stereoscope, through which the two notions may be seen, blent in the unity of a single conception? The defined idea of personality, and the shadowy notion of the infinite, may be bracketed together under a common term, which expresses them both; can they also be *thought* in conjunction? and have we any warrant for the inference that they actually coalesce in the supreme existence which we call God? This is the chief problem in the philosophy of theism.

In dealing with it, all that we seem warranted in affirming is, that personality is *one* of the characteristics under which the Supreme Being manifests himself; not that it is exhaustive of those phases of manifestation that are either possible or actual.   If we say that it is the highest aspect known to us. we speak in a figure, and proclaim the poverty of our insight. For, to the Infinite, there is nothing either high or low.   These are ratios of comparison by which the finite calculates. We give to the notion of personality an eminence and value that are unique; because, amongst the phenomena of the universe, it seems to us the noblest and the most commanding.   But it is not, of necessity, the exclusive idea attachable to the Divine Nature.   That, within the fullness of its infinitude, there should be aspects, phases, features, characteristics, which are totally unlike and utterly transcending the personality of which we are conscious, is a simple deduction from that infinitude.

With entire consistency, therefore, we may affirm at once the personality and the transcendency of God; that is to say, we may affirm that He is a person, as we understand the term, and that He is *more* than a person, as we understand it.   We cannot limit the aspects which his Being may assume to the phases which our own nature presents, any more than we may narrow the limits of his efficiency within the boundaries of our own. If we believe that everything distinctive of human personality exists in God, in more exalted phases, we must believe that infinitely more, at the same time different from it, co-exists within that nature. In other words, although we recognize certain features in the Divine infinitude, analogous to the personality of which we are conscious, it does not follow that we may identify the two, and take the human as a measure of the Divine. It is true we may err by taking a poor and circumscribed notion, gathered from the workings of our own faculties, and substituting it for the glory that is impersonal, and the order that is eternal; but that danger is not so great as is the counter-risk of losing the personal altogether in the nebulous haze of the infinite. The divine Absoluteness is lost to view, if we think merely of an infinite human being; and God is as truly discerned in the life, the movements, and the glory of the universe, which we cannot call human, — in the absolute Order, the eternal Beauty, the impersonal Sublimity, and the indefinite Splendor, which we can describe by no human attribute or tendency, — as He is revealed in the wisdom, the tenderness, the grace, and the affection that are properly our own.

Further, were we warranted in taking our human nature as the sole clue to the Divine, we might regard it also as its criterion or test ; and, carrying up its mingled moral phenomena, might find their archetypes in celestial tendencies to evil as well as to good. It is the notion that the sphere of finite existence supplies us with an area for inductive inference as to the procedure of the Absolute, that has given rise to so many of the distortions of popular theology.

What, then, is our warrant for assuming an *analogy* which does not amount to an *identity*, and in thus affirming the existence of a Personality at once real and transcendent, or — if we may venture on the distinction — human, yet not anthropomorphic ?

The radical feature of personality, as known to us — whether apprehended by self-consciousness or recognized in others — is the survival of a permanent self under all the fleeting or deciduous phases of experience ; in other words, the personal identity that is involved in the assertion,

" I am." While my individual thoughts, feelings, and acts pass away and perish, I continue to exist, to live, and to grow in the fullness of experience. Beneath the shows of things, the everlasting flux and reflux of phenomenal change, a substance or interior essence survives. Is limitation a necessary adjunct of *that* notion? May there not be an everlasting succession of thoughts, emotions, and volitions, — acts of consciousness in perpetual series, — while the substantial and permanent self remains, underneath the evanescent phenomena? and may not the thought, feeling, etc., have an infinite range, and be all-pervasive and interpenetrating at every spot within the universe? Surely limitation does not enter of necessity into the notion of personality. The *action* of a personal being is limited by the material on which he works, by his surroundings and circumstances; and our personalities are limited by other things, because they surround us; but if we surrounded them, and pervaded all finite things by omnipresent energy, the limitation would be simply a mode of action, and a condition of activity. It does not therefore follow, from our experience of limitation, that in being conscious, the conscious subject must be *invariably* or *necessarily* limited by the presence and environment of others. May it not be unlimited in act, unshackled by conditions, spontaneous in all it does, although it acts through the instrumentality and agency of others?

We may put the question in a fresh form thus : Is separateness from other existences equivalent to finitude? Does the one notion carry the other with it, or within it? All finite existences *are* separate, one from another ; but does it follow that all existence that is separate from other forms or phases must be finite? The infinite existence, which we conceive as the simple negation of the finite, may surely pervade the latter without limitation. The idea of a fence or boundary is not involved in the notion of Personality in the abstract, although it is involved in the notion of finite personality. It does not therefore follow that, if a being is personal, it must on that account be simply one out of many, — differentiated from others, by reason of its personality. Its personality need not be the cause of its separateness and differentiation. Doubtless it cannot exist out of relation to other beings; since — to fall back on the suggestions of philology — all *existence*, or the emergence of being in definite forms and relations, implies separateness from others. Although particular existence is what it is, however, in virtue of other existences determining and conditioning it, — and we, in our limitation, cannot be conscious of our own personality, except under the condition of a *non-ego* beyond us, — it is an illegitimate inference from this to affirm that personality cannot exist, or be consciously realized, except under the condition of a limiting *non-ego*. Is it not conceivable that the sense of a limiting *non-ego* would vanish, in the case of a being that was transcendent, and a life that was all-pervasive? That the dualism, involved in all finite consciousness, should cease in the case of the Infinite, may be difficult *for us* to realize; but to affirm that self-consciousness of necessity implies a centre or focus, at which the scattered rays of individuality are gathered up, is assuredly to transgress by the unwarranted use of a physical analogy.

I may here quote from Strauss, who always states his case with force and clearness :—

The modern monotheistic conception of God has two sides, that of the Absolute and that of the Personal, which, although united in Him, are so in the same manner as that in which two qualities are sometimes found in one person. one of which can be traced to the father's side, the other to the mother's. The one element is the Hebrew Christian, the other the Græco-philosophical contribution to our conception of God. We may say that we inherit from the Old Testament the " Lord-God," from the New the " God-Father," but from the Greek philosophy the " Godhead," or the " Absolute." [1]

So far well, and excellently put. But if it be so, if these notions — seemingly incompatible — are united in our modern monotheism " in the same manner as two qualities are sometimes found in one person," does not that mitigate the difficulty of realizing both as combined in one transcendent Personality? As two rills of hereditary influence unite to form a single stream of personality in the individual, and as two great conceptions of God have survived in

[1] *Old and New Faith*, p. 121.

the world, and alternately come to the front in the mind of the race, — call them, for distinction's sake, the Hebraic and the Hellenic, — cannot these be supposed to unite in one vast stream of Transcendent Being? And are not these two conceptions merely different ways of *interpreting* that supreme Existence, which both equally recognize? If we inherit these notions from the sources which Strauss so happily indicates, why should we proceed to disown one half of the inheritance, casting out the Jewish as airy and unverifiable, while we retain the Greek as real and scientific? If we are indebted to both, why refuse one half of the legacy? or construe it as the ghostly shadow? while the other is the enduring substance? Was not the monotheism of the Jew at least a historical discipline to the human consciousness, in the interpretation of a real side of the mystery, which in its fullness eluded him, as much as it baffled the Greek ontologists? Grant that the Jewish notion of personality degenerated at times into an anthropomorphism that was crude, and scarcely more elevated than the polytheism it supplanted. The emphasis which it laid on the distinction and separateness of God from the world was, nevertheless, part of the historic education of the race; just as the emphasis which the Greek mind laid on the unity which underlies all separateness was another part of that many-sided education.

The idea that "personality implies a limit" is largely due to the physical or semi-physical notions that have gathered round the notion of a throne on which a monarch is seated. If we give up these symbols of a "throne," a "court," and "a retinue of angels," and even renounce that of a local "heaven" as an "optical illusion," we shall not thus "lose every attribute of personal existence and action," as Strauss tells us we must. Every rational theist, nay every thoughtful man, understands that these ideas are the mere symbolical drapery, which has been wrapped around the spiritual notion by the realistic imagination of the Jews.

The whole of the sensuous imagery under which the Divine Nature is portrayed, as well as the material figures inlaid in every sentence in which we speak of the spiritual realm, are mere aids to the imaginative faculty. They are the steps of a ladder on which we rise, in order that we may transcend the symbols, — just as we find that a realization of indefinite areas of space, or intervals of time, helps us in that transcendent act, by which we think away the finite, and reach the infinite. But that God is, to quote the ancient formula, "all in the whole and all in every part" (as the soul is in the body), not localized at any centre, — this is one of the commonplaces of theology. The notion of the oriental mind, which has colored much of our western theology, that such symbols as those associated with royalty must be taken literally, and not as "figures of the true," is expressly rejected in some of the definitions of the Church itself. And further, there is scarcely an idea connected with the monotheism of the Jews — such as King, Judge, Lawgiver, Father — in reference to which there are not express statements, within the Sacred Books of the nation, cautioning it against a *literal* application of these terms to the Infinite. The prophets saw their inadequacy, and felt their poverty, while they used them. But they

could not help using them. They could
not speak to the mass of the nation in
other than symbolic language, any more
than the leaders of the Greek schools
could have dispensed with an esoteric, and
made the crowds in the agora understand
speculation on Being in the abstract. If
we are to speak of God at all in human
words, we must employ the inadequate
medium of metaphoric speech; and "jealousy to resist metaphor" does not, as
Francis Newman says, "testify to depth
of insight."[1] In their horror of anthropomorphism, ontologists have rarefied their
notion of the ultimate Principle of Existence into a mere abstraction, a blank
formless essence, a mere vacuum. But, in
making free use of anthropomorphic language, we know that it is of necessity
partial, and at the last inadequate; and we
exclude from our notion of personality —
which it thus imperfectly describes —
every anthropomorphic feature that savors
of limitation, while we retain the notion

[1] " To refuse to speak of God as loving and planning,
as grieving and sympathizing, without the protest of a
quasi, will not tend," he adds, "to clearer intellectual
views (for what can be darker?), but will muddy the
springs of affection." — *The Soul,* p. 29.

of a Being who is *personal and yet infinite.*

That personality cannot coexist with
infinity is an assumption without speculative warrant, or experiential proof. It
may be essential to personality that the
person " thinks and loves," as Mr. Arnold
puts it. But are thought and emotion
only susceptible of finite action, and adequate to accomplish finite ends? And, if
the stream to which they give rise is limited, may not the Fountain whence they
flow be infinite? Can we not realize the
existence of a Supreme Personality, within
which the whole Universe lives, moves,
and has its being and which has that universe as an area in which to manifest
its thought, feeling, and purpose? May
not the intelligence, traces of which we
see everywhere in the physical order, —
the purpose, in the manifestation of which
there is no gap or chasm anywhere, — be
the varying index of an omnipresent Personality? Into thought and emotion themselves the idea of restriction does not enter; although, whenever they appear in
special acts or concrete instances, they assume a finite form. They are then lim-

ited by each other, and by their opposites, as well as by every specific existence in which they respectively appear. But to themselves in the abstract the idea of limitation no more appertains than it is necessarily bound up with the notion of power or energy. This, however, is to anticipate.

We are deceived when we carry into the realm of Nature and the Infinite the analogy of a material centre and a physical circumference, by which our own personality is "cabined and confined." To the Infinite, there can be neither centre nor circumference; or we may say that the centre is everywhere, and the circumference nowhere. But if the attributes of mind or intelligence are revealed throughout the whole extent of the universe open to our inspection, is it impossible to conjoin with the notion of their infinite range the idea of a Person, to whom they belong, in whom they inhere, and of whose essence they are the many-sided manifestation? Is there any greater difficulty in supposing their conjunction over the whole universe than in realizing their coincidence at any one spot within it?

It is assuredly not the mere extent of the area that constitutes the difficulty of their union.

We thus come back to what has, in some form or another, lain at the root of every theistic argument. Is the universe in any sense intelligible? Can it be read, understood, and interpreted by us at all? or does it present an " untranslatable text," which we in vain attempt to decipher? When we say that phenomena are *organized*, what do we mean by the statement? When we speak of them as correlated, reciprocal, ordered, the parts of a whole, what do we mean by these terms? Are we projecting our own thoughts outwards, on the face of external nature? or are we engaged in deciphering an inscription that is written there? Surely, in the earliest and simplest act of perception, distinguishing one phenomenon from another, we recognize the presence of mind within the universe; and in our earliest knowledge of an external world, we have an experience suggesting the theistic inference.

One solution of the problem of theism may thus be found in the answer we give to the question, Are we warranted in interpreting the universe in the light of our own intelligence? We are accustomed to think, both popularly and scientifically, that we know something of Nature ; and we coördinate our knowledge in the several sciences. But all the sciences take for granted a general doctrine of the knowable, and they all start from the presupposition that in constructing them we do not merely project our own thought into Nature, but discover something regarding natural phenomena themselves. We speak as aimlessly in our most exact and scientific language as if we talked at random, if we do not find thought and reason within all natural phenomena, as their substrate, their essence, or their presupposition. Even if we assume the *rôle* of the agnostic, and take refuge in a confession of ignorance, under the seeming modesty which disclaims insight, a latent doctrine of knowledge is nevertheless involved. If we hold that all knowledge reaches us through the senses, that we can attain to nothing higher than "transformed sensations," still behind this theory of the origin of our ideas there lies an uneliminable element which transcends it, and which is unconsciously taken for granted in every theoretical explanation of things as they are. If, therefore, mind be visible in nature, and we cannot construe a single phenomenon or group of phenomena otherwise than in terms of intelligence, our interpretation is not the result of unconscious idealization. It is the discernment of objective reality, and is also the recognition of mind, in the process of manifestation.

Finding, therefore, the signs of mind everywhere, in the correlations and successions of phenomena, may we not interpret the whole series as the manifestation of a personal entity underlying it? Of a mind that is impersonal we cannot form a notion. Do not all the forms of finite being, therefore, — the specializations of existence and the successions of phenomena — lead to the conclusion that there is a Supreme Essence in which every specialization is blent, a whole in which all succession is merged? Do not the successive parts lead the mind to a "unity, where no division is?" And if we thus interpret individual and fragmentary things in terms of intel-

ligence, surely we cannot dispense with
Mind, when we rise to that supreme unity
in which variety ceases, and multiplicity is
lost to view.

It must be admitted that we do not know
what constitutes the inmost essence of personality, under all the shifting phases of experience ; and, on that account, there is an
element of vagueness attaching to the idea.
But we are aware that our own identity
or self-hood survives, while the successive
waves of experience rise and fall ; and, it is
surely quite conceivable that the eternal
Essence or everlasting Substance of the
Universe should be supremely conscious of
self, throughout all the change and turmoil
of existence.   It may be that infinitude
alone supplies the condition for a perfect
consciousness of personality ; and that our
finiteness, as Lotze thinks, is "not a productive condition of personality, but rather
a hindering barrier to its perfect development."[1]   If there is a difficulty in thus
conceiving of a personality which can dispense with a *non-ego,* as the condition of its
activity, — which does not necessarily involve the distinction between self and not-

[1] *Microcosmus*, iii. p. 575.

self, — and if, in consequence, we are unable to compress our belief in the Divine Personality within the mould of a logical formula, "let it" (as Mr. Greg says of the belief in immortality), "let it rest in the vague, if you would have it rest unshaken. It is maintainable so long as it is suffered to remain nebulous and unoutlined." The very grandeur of the term "God" consists in the fact that it includes not less, but so much more, than any specific description could embrace within it. The reality surpasses every definition of it ; and our various theoretical explanations of the fact — which appeals to our consciousness in forms so manifold — are just so many ways by which we successively register our own imperfect and changeful insight. We put into intelligible shape a conviction which, the moment we define it, is felt to transcend our definitions immeasurably.

But are our definitions ever correct ? In answer to this we may affirm that they are accurate so far as they go, while admittedly incomplete. They need not lay claim to be either final or exhaustive of that which they endeavor to define. At the very best they are the result of the efforts of the reason to formulate a conviction which has several distinct roots, and assumes many different phases, but which is not invariable, or steadily luminous, or always irresistible. From the very nature of the case, the Divine Personality must be *suggested*, rather than evidenced with indubitable force ; and if we can, by reason, scatter the *a priori* difficulties which seem to gather round the notion itself, it may be left to the workings of intuition to reveal the positive fact, *a posteriori*, in the flash of occasional inspiration. If the Divine Presence were obtruded upon the inward eye, as material objects appeal to the sense of sight, the faculties which recognize it would be dazzled, and unable to note or register anything besides. Our recognition of God must therefore be casual, fugitive, occasional, to leave room for our knowledge of, and our relation to, other things. Were it continuous and uniform, it would sink to the level of our consciousness of finite things and material existence. Perhaps, in its very fugitiveness and transiency there may be evidence of its divineness ; and that there should be endless discussion, and the perpetual shock of controversy in regard to it, it is only to be expected. If the aspects under which the Infinite is revealed vary perpetually, if He at once surrounds and pervades us, yet withdraws from our gaze, the everlasting controversy of the ages, and the rise and fall of systems which now assert and now dispense with his presence, are most easily explained. The perpetual resuscitation of debate (after solutions have been advanced by the score) is proof of the working of an instinct which rises higher than the proofs themselves. They are, all of them, — the ontological, cosmological, teleological, and the rest, — merely historical memorials of the efforts of the human mind *to vindicate to itself the existence of a reality of which it is conscious, but which it cannot perfectly define.* In their completest forms, they are the result of the activity of the reason and the conscience combined, to account for that reality, and to define it to others.

That our consciousness of the Divine Personality is often dormant says nothing against its genuineness or trustworthiness, when stirred to life. It rather tells the other way. What is ceaselessly obtruded on our notice is not more true, by reason of its obviousness, than what is flashed upon us in moments of transient ecstasy or insight. We are not always on the mountain-tops; nor can we breathe the ethereal air forever, or live in the white light of a never-ceasing apocalypse. But these are surely the supreme moments of discernment. Could any one rationally affirm that the dull flats of mental life — in which our powers are arrested and distracted by a multiplicity of objects surrounding them, our thoughts embarrassed by contingency and change — are more significant of the truth of things than those in which our faculties are kindled into life by the sense of a stupendous Presence appealing to them, and yet concealing itself from their scrutiny? Nor will the general consciousness of the race admit that the later are times of mere idealistic trance and poetic illusion. Rather are they times of inspiration, in which we see beyond appearances, and beneath all semblance, into the inner life of things.

The question has so many sides that, at the risk of some repetition, it may be restated thus: It is said that limitation is involved in all activity, and that, if there

be an infinite Personality, it is doomed
to everlasting repose, without act or sign
of energy; for to act is to be limited by
the conditions of activity. Thus each specific mode of energy which takes shape
in a determinate form is, *ipso facto*, cur-
tailed. Power emerging from its latent
state, and *showing itself* on the theatre of
finite existence, limits itself, by its very
relation, to the things on which it oper-
ates. Therefore it is only the indetermi-
nate that can be unlimited and infinite.
This is the difficulty.

But, in the first place, is not power in its
latent state — *i. e.*, unmanifested, or spe-
cialized in a concrete form — more limited
in its retirement, and hampered by its se-
clusion, than it would be in its energy and
activity? *Character* is not limited by the
special acts in which it is revealed. On
the contrary, the more varied its features,
the greater and fuller is the character. It
is not the absence of definite characteristics
that proves one human nature to be richer
than another, but their number, their intensity, their manifoldness, and their range.

In the second place, a limit may be
self-imposed; and if so, it is simply one

of the conditions under which alone power can manifest itself. Resistance reveals power, by giving an opportunity for energy to overcome the barrier. Power unresisted is power unmanifested, and may be conceived of as latent heat ; but it is the presence of some obstacle to be overcome which shows the power of that which subdues it, in the very act of yielding and being overthrown. It may be conceded that whenever power is exercised, and issues in a definite act, it is limited by its relation to other acts. It immediately becomes one of the million links, in the chain of finite things. But the fountain-head of energy, whence the act has come forth to play its part in the theatre of existence, is unaffected by that limitation. In short, the act may be limited, while the Agent is not.

In the third place, the actual conditions under which we live, and under which our personality works, prove that the existence of a barrier in some directions enlarges, deepens, and widens our personality in others (take, for example, the limitation or restriction involved in all duty). And this enlargement is not due merely to the law of compensation, and to the fact that what is lost on one side is gained on another; but it is because, without the limit or the constraint, the highest form of activity could not possibly exist.

Perhaps, however, the main speculative difficulty is experienced, not when we attempt to construe to our minds the existence of the Divine Personality alone, but when we try to conceive it in its relation to humanity; when we endeavor, in fact, to realize the *coexistence* of the Infinite with the finite. So long as we think only of the Infinite, there is no logical puzzle, and the intellectually consistent scheme of pantheism emerges; so long, again, as we think only of the finite, there is no dilemma, though we seem locked in the embrace of an atheistic system. But try to combine the infinite with the finite — the former being not the mere expansion of the latter, but its direct negation — and, in the dualism which their union forces upon us, a grave difficulty seems to lurk. What relation do the innumerable creatures that exist bear to the all-surrounding and all-pervading Essence? It cannot be similar to that which the planets bear to the sun, round which they revolve ; for the sun is only a vaster finite, like its satellites : and God + the universe is not a sum of being, equivalent to that of the sun + the planetary bodies. How, then, can there be two substances, a finite and an infinite ? Does not the latter necessarily quench the former by its very presence ? As a child of four years once put it to me, " If God is everywhere, how is there any room for us ? "

We must admit that if God be "the sum of all reality" (as the Eleatics, the later Platonists, Erigena, Spinoza, and Hegel have maintained), then, since we are a part of that sum, we are necessarily included within the Divine Essence. Further, if there be but one substance in the universe, and all the phenomena of the human consciousness, together with those of the external world, are but the varying phases which that single reality assumes ; then, it matters not what we call it, — a force, a cause, a person, a substance, a life, God, — all that *is*, is *of it*. This is the pantheistic solution of the problem, which has fascinated so many of the subtlest minds. It has, of course, been met by the doctrine of creation in time, or the origination of finite existence at a particular instant by the fiat of a Creator. Many believe that this doctrine is essential to theism, and are afraid that if we allow a perpetual cosmos, we must dispense with an eternal God, except as an *opifex mundi;* that if we do not affirm the origin of the universe *ex nihilo*, we are unable to maintain the separateness of God from it, and his transcendency.

I see no warrant for this. To affirm that without an absolute start of existence out of blank nonentity into manifested being, we have no evidence of God at all, or only the signs of an eternally hampered Deity, — a mere supplement to the sum of existence, — is altogether illegitimate. For the evidence of Divine action would then be dependent on the signs of past effort, or the occurrence of some stupendous stroke, crisis, or burst of energy. Why may not the story of the universe be rather interpreted as *the everlasting effect of an eternal Cause?* Do we need an origin in time, if we have a perpetual genesis, or a ceaseless becoming, coeval with the everlasting cause? Which is the grander, which the more realizable notion, to suppose Nature at one moment non-existent, and the next "flashed into material reality at the fiat of Deity;" or to suppose it eternally plastic under the power of an Artificer, who is perpetually fashioning it, through all the cycles of progressive change? It is not the actual entrance or the possible exit of existence that we have to explain, but its manipulations, the rise of organizations and their decay, the evolution and succession of varied types of life; and it is precisely these which attest the presence of an indwelling and immediately acting God.

Dualism, therefore, finds its speculative warrant, not in any assumed act of creation, but in the eternal necessities of the case, in the double element involved in all knowledge, and such experiential facts as those of sense - perception and intuition generally.

To get rid of the dualism of monotheistic theory, which seemed to him to limit the Infinite, Spinoza adopted the old monistic position; holding God and nature to be but the eternal cause and the everlasting effect, *natura naturans* and *natura naturata*. This theory, however, affords

no explanation of how the mind of man
blossoms into a consciousness of the Infinite, of how the finite knower reaches his
conception of the Infinite ; because, according to the theory, all that is reached
by the mind of the knower is itself a development of the infinite. The psychological act of recognition is itself only a wave
on the sea of existence. Dualism explains
the apprehension of the one by the other,
in its affirmation that all our knowledge
is obtained under the conditions of contrast and difference, and thus reaches us
in pairs of opposites. It does not affirm
that, in order to the consciousness of personality in the Infinite, there must of necessity be a recognition of self and not-
self, of self and the universe ; but it affirms
that to the finite knower it must be so ;
that to him subject implies object, and the
ego the *non-ego;* that the two are given
together, and are realizable only in union.

On every monistic theory of the universe, however, the question, "Where is
God to be found?" is meaningless. A
"search for God" is a contradiction in
terms ; because the seeker and the search,
the quest and the *quæsitor* and the *quæsi-*

tum, are all manifestations of one and the same substance. Dualism is involved in the very notion of a search.

Further, to take for granted that the Infinite is that which quenches the finite, which abolishes and absorbs it, is to beg the whole question in debate. This super-session of the finite by the Infinite is speculatively as illegitimate as is the acosmism of Spinoza. It is true that we reach the *idea* of the infinite by removing the finite out of the way. But then the act of exclusion or absorption, being an act of thought, constitutes one term of a re-lation. If we can think of the infinite at all, we have a mental concept which stands contrasted with that of the finite, and thus again dualism emerges. Al-though our conception of the infinite is reached by the abolition of the finite, it does not follow that if an Infinite Being exists, the finite can coexist with it. For, the latter is not only given as a prior fact of consciousness, but, when we proceed to eliminate it, the act of thinking it away, being finite, supplies us with the unelim-inable element of dualistic relation and difference. Further, if it be true that to predicate anything whatever of the infinite is to assign a limit to it, — if the maxim *omnis determinatio est negatio* be sound, — then the infinite has to the human mind no definite meaning whatsoever. It is not distinguishable from the non-existent ; and the conclusion, "being = nothing," is reached. Hegel himself admits that "abstract supersensible essence, void of all difference and all specific character, is a mere *caput mortuum* of the abstract understanding."[1] But on what principle are we debarred from claiming for the Infinite Essence, simply because of its infinity, all possible, all conceivable predicates, and therefore the power of revealing itself to the finite knower. To affirm the opposite is not to limit us alone, it is to limit the Infinite by denying its power of self-manifestation.

In all thought and consciousness dualism emerges because there is invariably a subject and an object, a knower and a thing known. But do these limit each other? How so? We know in part ; but the object we discern may be recognized by us as infinite, in the very act of knowing it in

<hr>

[1] *Logic,* § 112.

part. We may be aware that what we apprehend transcends, in its inmost nature, our apprehension of it; while the latter fact does not abolish the former, or reduce our supposed knowledge to ignorance. While, therefore, all knowledge enters the mind under dualistic conditions, this psychological fact does not relegate the object known by us to the category of the finite, or prevent the direct knowledge of God in his infinity and transcendency. Nor does it follow that, with a double element in all cognition, one of the two must be positive and the other negative, as some of the advocates of nescience contend. They may both be equally positive and negative, since each is antithetic of the other, and is nevertheless its supporting background in the field of consciousness. One of the two may be prominent at a particular moment, but the other is invariably present behind it, giving it form and character. In other words, the relativity of human apprehension does not cut us off from a direct and positive knowledge of the Infinite. As it is admirably put by Dr. Martineau, "We admit the relative character of human thought

as a psychological fact : we deny it as an
ontological disqualification." [1]

The most direct suggestions of personality in alliance with infinity reach us through the channel of the moral faculty. They are disclosed in the phenomena of conscience, and also of affection.

Before indicating how these suggestions arise, I return to the teaching of Mr. Arnold on the subject. He has made us all so much his debtors by the light he has cast on sundry historical problems, and his rare literary skill in handling these, that any critic of his work, who differs from him on so radical a point as the nature of God, finds the task neither easy nor congenial. In addition to the obscurity which the subject itself presents, there is a special difficulty in adequately estimating a writer, whose criticism is on most points so true, so subtle, and profound.

Admiration, however, is one thing ; assent is another. Mr. Arnold wishes us to use the Bible fruitfully, and his contributions to its fruitful use have been neither few nor slight. Nevertheless, in his attack on what he terms the " God of metaphys-

1 *Essays Philosophical and Theological*, p. 234.

ics," in his elaborate critical assault —
lacking neither in "vigor nor in rigor" —
on the notion of Personality in God, he re-
moves, as it seems to me, the very basis of
theology ; and the whole superstructure of
the science becomes fantastic and unreal.
He is sanguine of laying the basis of a
"religion more serious, potent, awe-inspiring, and profound than any which the
world has yet seen " (p. 109), but he builds
it on the ruins of the theistic philosophy
of the past. The latter must in the first
instance be leveled with the ground, and
the *débris* removed. We are to find "the
elements of a religion — new, indeed, but
in the highest degree hopeful, solemn, and
profound " (p. 109) — only when we renounce the delusion that " God is a person who thinks and loves," regarding it as
a " fairy tale," as " figure and personification," and of the same scientific value as
the personification of the sun or the wind.

Religion, however, being the expression
of dependence, involves and carries with
it the recognition of an Object on whom
the worshiper depends ; and, as he is personal, and his personality is most distinctly evinced in his religion, the Object

on whom he depends, and whom he recognizes, must be personal also. Without personality — or its archetype and analogue — in God, religion is reduced to a poetic thrill or glow of emotion. If recognition is absent from it, it is not only blind and deaf and dumb, it is also inarticulate and vague. But, as was happily said of the system of Comte, "the wine of the real presence being poured out," we are asked "to adore the empty cup."

The readers of Mr. Arnold do not need to be told that Speculative Philosophy — in the grand historic use and wont of the term — is to him a barren region, void of all human interest ; and that intellectual travel over it is pronounced by him to be resultless. His dismissal of the metaphysical arguments for Divine Personality, "with sheer satisfaction" "because they have convinced no one, have given rest to no one, have given joy to no one, nay, no one has even really understood them" (pp. 104, 105), is curious as coming from so distinguished an advocate of rich and many-sided culture. Curious, — when one remembers that from the schools of Speculative Philosophy all the great movements of opinion in other departments have originally sprung, and that every question raised in these departments must ultimately run up into the region of metaphysic. On a first perusal of Mr. Arnold's delightful papers, one feels that he is being led, by the most charming of guides, into the regions of light and of certitude. By and by he finds that his guide is an army-leader, who intends "boldly to carry the war into the enemy's country, and see how many strong fortresses of the metaphysicians he can enter and rifle" (p. 96). He becomes the general in a new crusade against our English notions about God, our crass metaphysics, and our unverifiable theology, and would prepare the way for a "religion more serious, potent, awe-inspiring, and profound than any which the world has yet seen" by first cleverly chaffing the old philosophy out of the way.

But this disparagement of the whole region of metaphysic, because it deals with the questions of "being" and "essence," is not so surprising as is Mr. Arnold's attempt to find, in the simple etymology of words, a clue to the mysteries which baffle the ontologist. In this investigation, interesting as it is, he has started on a journey which ends in a *cul de sac*. To discover the origin of the terms Being, Essence, Substance, by getting hold of the primitive Aryan root whence the Greek, Latin, French, or English words have been derived, will not help us in the inquiry which concerns the origin of the ideas expressed by these terms. *Abstracta ex concretis* may be the law of linguistic derivation; and, by etymological study, we may learn how the human race has come to make use of certain terms, and to attach particular meanings to them. In following the course of the ancient river of linguistic affinity, we may trace the process by which the notions of movement, growth, and permanence have possibly grown out of the "breathe," "grow," and "stand" of the old Aryan root. But the most exact knowledge of the subtlest windings of this river will not solve, will not even give us the materials for solving, the ulterior question, whether the human mind has imaginatively transformed the concrete into the abstract, or has been all the while interpreting to itself an objective reality.

"By a simple figure," says Mr. Arnold,

"these terms declare a perceived energy and operation, nothing more. Of a subject, that performs this operation, they tell us nothing" (p. 82). These "primitives" have been "falsely supposed to bring us news about the primal nature of things, to declare a subject in which inhered the energy and operation we had noticed, to indicate a fontal category, or supreme constitutive condition, into which the nature of all things whatsoever might be finally run up" (p. 82). No one, so far as I am aware, has maintained this, as Mr. Arnold puts it. Let it be conceded that our abstract terms arose out of concretes; that, as acts of perception must have preceded the processes of generalization in the race (as they precede them in the experience of each individual), the words employed to express abstract ideas were first used to describe individual or concrete things ; and that, the etymological research, which unravels for us the intricate processes of growth, adaptation, and change, in the *usus loquendi* of terms, is one of the most fruitful branches of inquiry. But, supposing the entire course of linguistic development traced for us by an unerring hand, and in precise scientific detail, the whole question will reemerge, and confront us as before, What has the human mind really done, in making use of these concrete terms to express its abstract notions? To express them at all, it must use *some* word; and that it selects one, which originally described an individual or concrete thing, tells nothing against the fact that it is now able to abstract from these particulars, and to describe, by means of the adopted term, ideas which have not entered the mind by the gateway of the senses.

Mr. Arnold speaks of the words "is" and "be" as "mysterious petrifactions which remain in language as if they were autochthons there, as if no one could go beyond them or behind them. Without father, without mother, without descent, as it seemed, they yet are omnipresent in our speech, and indispensable" (p. 83); whereas he has shown that the terms really arose out of our sense-experience of concrete things. Let us suppose that he is correct in his account of the process by which the product has been reached. He merely exhibits to us a genealogical chart. or tree of derivation. A out of B, B out of C, C

out of X.   But the real question lies behind the genealogy.   We may imagine our
Aryan forefathers, in their infantile gaze
over the ever-changing world of phenomena, describing what met the eye and ear
and senses generally, by certain words,
mostly imitative of the sounds of nature.
Then, as their intelligence grew — with the
repetition of the old, and the occurrence
of new experience, — if they wished to express the notion of a thing existing, they
made use of a term which they had previously used to describe its operation, viz.,
"breathing."   Were this statement of the
origin and prehistoric use of abstract terms
found to be correct, — a point which must
be determined by specialists in the domain
of archaic etymology, — the investigation
would not have guided us one step towards
the solution of the graver problem, as to
the origin of the ideas with which the terms
deal.   We would have been merely moving
on the surface-plane of phenomenal succession, and the most accurate account of that
process would no more explain the source
of the ideas to which the mind has affixed
the old terms, than the discovery of all the
links of a chain would explain its origin
or method of construction.

Mr. Arnold would persuade us that, because the terms which now describe our abstract categories were originally used to describe objects known by sense-perception, the ideas came in also by that outward gateway. Is it not a better explanation of these "mysterious petrifactions," *is* and *be*, that the notions which they represent, the categories which they describe, are themselves autochthons in the human mind; and that they spring up out of the soil of consciousness, whenever that soil is made ready for their growth, by the scantiest intellectual husbandry? Indigenous to the spirit of man, — though latent in its inmost substance till evolved by the struggle of mind with its environment, — it is not surprising that in afterwards naming them, the simple words, once used to describe the operations of nature, or of man, should be invested with new meanings ; or that in the course of ages they should have broadened out into general and abstract terms.

But if neither the etymology of particular words, nor a study of the origin and growth of language, affords us any help in determining the origin of our ideas, it is equally certain that no knowledge of "pre-

historic man " can aid us in solving that
ulterior question. Suppose it proved that
man has arisen, in the long struggle for
existence, out of elements inferior to himself, and that his present beliefs have been
evolved out of lower phases of thought and
feeling, this proof will not determine — it
will not even touch — the problem of the
reality of that existence, to which the
present beliefs of the race bear witness.
The question of chief interest is not the
genealogical one, of how we have come to
be endowed with these beliefs, but the
metaphysical one, of their present validity
to the individual and to the species. Are
they, as they now exist, competent wit-
nesses to an outstanding fact and an abiding reality? It matters little how a belief has been reached, if its final verdict be
true ; and the method of its development
casts no light on the intrinsic character,
or the trustworthiness of its attestations.
The evolution of organic existence out of
the inorganic, and of the rational out of the
organic — supposing it scientifically demonstrated, and every missing link in the
chain of derivation supplied — would only
tell us of a law, or method, or process of

becoming. It would give us no information as to the nature of the Fountain-head, out of which the stream of development has flowed, and is flowing now. What has been evolved, in the slow uprise and growth of innumerable ages, is the outcome of an

Eternal process moving on

in lines of continuous succession, — an ever-advancing stream of physical, intellectual, and moral tendency. But the question remains, Is this onward movement a real advance? Is it progressive, as well as successive? Are the later conceptions of the universe — which have been developed out of the guesses of primeval men — really "higher," because more accurate, interpretations of the reality of things? Or, is the whole series of notions from first to last an illusory process of idealization and personification, and therefore mere conjecture and guess-work? Grant that theology has grown out of nature-worship; has the growth been a progressive, and progressively accurate, interpretation of what is? If the conception of a spiritual Presence has emerged out of the animal sensations of childhood, and the subtlest analyses of

our Western theology have sprung out of
the fantastic notions of primitive religion,
the question of absorbing interest lies behind this, and is altogether unaffected by
it.   That question is, — Are our present
adult notions like a mirage in the desert,
or like

> The clouds that gather round the setting sun,

half the glory of which lies in the changefulness of their form and hue? or has the
race had an intuition of reality — varying
in accuracy, yet valid and authentic — at
each stage of its progress?   If the latter
alternative be rejected, in what has the advance consisted?   Surely there has been
no intelligible advance at all? and the
guesses of the child, at the foot of the
ladder of inquiry, have an equal scientific
value with the surmises of the most edu-
cated at the top; that is to say, neither
have any scientific value at all.

If there be any meaning in a rudimentary stage of human history, when the
notions formed of the universe were chaotic and distorted, and if this gave place
by gradual steps to a time when "the
ideas of conduct or moral order and right

had gathered strength enough to establish and declare themselves" (p. 135), what meaning are we to attach to the progress, unless in the latter period there was *a more accurate reading of the objective reality of things?* "The native, continuous, and increasing pressure upon Israel's spirit of the ideas of conduct, and its sanctions," Mr. Arnold calls "his intuition of the eternal that makes for righteousness." But whence came this pressure, this appeal from without, this solicitation and revelation? All that we are told is that "Israel had an intuitive faculty, a natural bent for these ideas" (p. 139). But the scientific investigator of the laws of historic continuity at once raises the farther question of whence? and how? Whence came they? and how did they originate? If these things pressed upon the national mind of Israel, it must either have been through tradition, the unconscious heritage of past experience working in the blood of the people, or through an eternally present Power, disclosing itself to the Hebraic race in a series of historic manifestations. But does an inferior state ever create a superior one? It necessarily precedes it in time. But is the lower ever causal of the higher? We are told that the "usage of the minority gradually became the usage of the majority" (p. 147). So far, we are simply recording facts which have occurred. We are dealing with history, with the successions of phenomena ; but we are explaining nothing.

Now, Philosophy essays an explanation of History. It is not satisfied with statistics. If we ask how the selfish and wholly animal tendencies of primitive society gradually gave place to others that were generous or elevated, — and if, in answer, we are merely directed to habit, custom, or usage, — it is evident that our director is simply veiling our ignorance from us, by a repetition of the question proposed. It is *an explanation* of the usage, not a restatement of it, that we desire. Habit merely tells us that a thing done once was repeated, and will be done again. What we want to know is, how it came to be repeated ? why it was done again ? why it was done at all ? How the bent of the race was determined this way rather than that — in favor of righteousness rather than its opposite — is therefore altogether unexplained by custom and association. It is the custom, association, and usage, that call for explanation. May not the existence of an eternally righteous Source, or Centre of the universe, explain it? The spirit of man can surely discern a supreme moral principle, if he himself stands in a close personal relation to it. And the rise from rudimentary perceptions to a state which we now agree to call the "moral order" — with the sanctions of society superadded to the customs of our ancestors — is on any other theory unaccountable.

In other words, we cannot validly affirm that the process of evolution has, after long conflict, brought to the front principles of conduct, which can be called the real elements of moral order, or of the constitution of society, if these have not proceeded from, and are the progressive manifestations of, an eternal moral Nature. If they are the product of a blind strife amongst rival tendencies, at what point do they become a rule for posterity? At what stage of evolution are we warranted in saying that "the perception, and the rule founded on it, have become a conquest forever, placing human nature on a higher stage ; so that, however much the perception and the rule may have been dubious and unfounded once, they must be taken to be certain and formed now?" (p. 153). At no stage could this be affirmed, because what has been formed by strife must alter with the continued action of the forces that have made it what it is. The child of contingency remains contingent, and may itself become the parent of endless future change. Unless, therefore, the law of evolution ceases to operate, and the process of development abruptly closes, the possible alteration of the canons of morality, after the conquest has been made, is not only as conceivable as it was before the struggle commenced, but it is as certain. Nay, the disappearance of these canons before some future rule of life is involved in their very origin, if that origin be merely the "survival of the fittest" in the long struggle for existence.

To put it otherwise. Let us suppose that the family bond arose out of the selfish struggles of primitive man, — that reverence for parents and love for children have been slowly evolved out of tendencies that were originally self-regarding, — why

should we call the later stage a more perfect one, for the race at large? It may be
more perfect, for those who have attained
to it ; but it would have been out of place,
if earlier in the field. Is it not an essential part of the process of development
that every stage is as necessary and as perfect as all its antecedent and all its subsequent stages? Unless a point is reached
when conduct becomes intrinsically excellent, — *excellent in virtue of its conformity
to a rule which is not the product of evolution, and which cannot be superseded by anything to be evolved millenniums hence*, —
how can we speak of monogamy and self-
restraint as "the true law of our being"
in contrast with the earlier promiscuous-
ness which it succeeded? Evolution, in
short, tells us nothing of a moral goal, because it gives us no information of a moral
Source. It supplies us with no standard,
because it points to no Centre ; and it
brings with it no ethical sanction higher
than custom, at any stage. *It has come
about* is all that it tells us of any phenomenon.

Now, not to speak of the fluctuating
moral verdicts of the world, and the obsti-

nate reversions from later to earlier standards, — that which has stood at the front
and dominated for a while, falling again to
the rear and being disregarded, — how can
we speak of one stage of human progress
as dim and rudimentary, and of another as
disciplined and mature, if there be no absolute standard towards which the efforts
of the race are tending, and should tend?
It is not merely that the ethical habit of
to-day may not be a "conquest forever,"
but only a chance victory in the skirmish
of circumstance, which the next great conflict may reverse. It is much more than
this. If the later state be the creation of
the former, and evolved out of it, — all the
stages being of equal value as cause and
consequence, — the very notion of an ethical struggle disappears. The successive
moments of moral experience are reduced
to the mere category of states, prior and
posterior, in the stream of development;
and conscious effort to reach a higher
standard, or to realize a nobler life, becomes unnatural discontent. It might
even be construed as rebellion against the
leadings of instinct! and, if so, the actual
would legitimately crush out the ideal.

Then, with the stimulus of aspiration gone, and the sense of control removed, the drift of the average man, and of the race, would be towards the easiest pleasures, and the satisfactions of the savage state.

The emergence of the conscience is one thing, its *creation* is another. Its rise out of lower elements, its consequent flexibility, and its possible transformation in the course of ages into a much more delicate instrument, — sensitive to all passing lights and shades and fine issues of conduct, — is perfectly consistent with its being a competent witness to a Reality, which it has gradually succeeded in apprehending, and which it has not merely idealized out of its own subjective processes. If the sentiment of duty arose out of an experience, which was at first as entirely devoid of it as that of the

> Baby new to earth and sky,

who

> Never thinks that this is I,

the obscure genesis of those convictions, which finally assume shapes so transcendent, could not invalidate or even affect their trustworthiness.

The story of the race is but the story

of the individual "writ large." When the moral sense awakens in a child, under the tutelage of its seniors, the influences to which it is subjected do not create its conscience. They merely evoke it. The child opens its eyes, and sees; although the process of learning to see accurately may be a much longer one in moral than in visual perception. If it is so with the child, why may it not be so similarly with the race? Why not *necessarily?* Let the processes of growth, therefore, be what they may, the source of the moral faculty lies hid beyond the lines of historical investigation, and the authority of the developed product is not invalidated by the discovery of its lineage.

It comes to this, that in the phenomena of conscience we find the traces of a principle

Deep-seated in our mystic frame,

which is not evolved out of the lower elements of appetency and desire. These phenomena disclose results, which are best explained by the presence of an *alter ego*, "in us, yet not of us." We can trace it working within, yet mysteriously overshadowing us, and suggesting — in the occasional flashes of light sent across the darker background of experience — the action of another Personality, *behind our own.*

Our account of the phenomena of conscience is not exhausted when we affirm that certain moral causes, set in operation by ourselves or others, issue in certain subjective effects upon the character. To say that definite consequences result from specific acts is only to state one half of the case, and that the least important half. How are our actions invested with the character of blameworthiness, or the reverse? Moral worth and baseness are not only two points or stages, in the upward or downward stream of tendency. The merit and the demerit are respectively due to the character of the stream, as determined at the moment, by the act and choice of the individual.

It is unnecessary at this point to raise the large question of the freedom of the will, its moral autonomy. It is enough to affirm that the theoretical denial of freedom will always be met by a counter affirmation, springing from a region unaffected by inductive evidence. It will also be met

by the recoil of the feelings of mankind
. from the doctrine of non-responsibility for
action, which is the logical outcome of that
denial. It may be safely affirmed that,
allowing for hereditary tendency, and the
influence of constraining circumstances,
the human race will continue to apportion
its praise and its blame to individuals, on
the ground that their action might take
shape in either of two contrary directions,
according to the choice and determination
of the will. No action ever arises absolutely *de novo*, unaffected by antecedent
causes, both active and latent; neither is
any action absolutely determined from
without, or from behind. In each act of
choice, the causal nexus remains unsev-
ered; while the act itself is ethically free,
and undetermined. In other words, affirming the moral autonomy of the will,
we deny the liberty of libertarian indifference; and affirming the integrity of the
causal nexus, we reject the despotism of
necessitarian fate: and we maintain that,
in so doing, we are not affirming and denying the same thing at the same time; but
that we are true to the facts of consciousness, and preserve a moral eclecticism,

which shuns "the falsehood of extremes," and has its evidence in the personality of the agent. The two rival schemes of Liberty and Necessity, both "resistless in assault, but impotent in defense," are practically overthrown by the ease with which each annihilates the other. To exhibit the *rationale* of this would require a long chapter.

Leaving it, therefore, — and assuming the freedom which we make no attempt to demonstrate, — the specialty of that Power which presides over the region of mixed motive and variable choice is at once its absoluteness, and its independence of the individual. It announces itself, in Kantian phrase, as the "categorical imperative." It is not ours, as an emotion or passion is ours. We speak in a figure of the *voice* of the conscience; implying, in our popular use of the term, its independence of us. It is not our own voice ; or, if the voice of the higher self, — in contrast with the lower, which it controls, — it is an inspiration in us, the whispered suggestion of a monitor "throned within our other powers." If it were merely the remonstrance of one part of our nature against the workings of another part, we might question its right to do more than claim to be an equal inmate of the house. In any case disregard of it would amount to nothing more serious than a loss of harmony, a false note marring the music of human action, or a flaw in argument that disarranged the sequences of thought. In the moral imperative, however, which commands us categorically, and acts without our order, and cannot be silenced by us, we find the hints of a Personality that is girding and enfolding ours. As admirably expressed by Francis Newman, —

This energy of life within is ours, yet it is not we.
It is in us, it belongs to us, yet we cannot control it.
It acts without our bidding, and when we do not think
    of it.
Nor will it cease its acting at our command, or other-
    wise obey us.
But while it recalls from evil, and reproaches us for evil,
And is not silenced by our effort, surely it is not *we* ;
Yet it pervades mankind, as one life pervades the trees.[1]

It is not that in the restraints of law we are conscious of a fence or boundary laid down by statute. But, in the most deli-

---

[1] *Theism*, p. 13. Cf. Fénelon. *De l'Existence de Dieu*, Part I. c. 1, § 29. See also Cardinal Newman, *Grammar of Assent*, Part I. c 5, § 1.

cate suggestions and surmises of this monitor, we are aware of a Presence " besetting
us " — as the Hebrews put it — " behind
and before," penetrating the soul, pressing
its appeals upon us, yet withdrawing itself
the moment it has uttered its voice, and
leaving us to the exercise of our own freedom. The most significant fact — if not
the most noticeable — in the relation of the
Conscience to the Will is its quick suggestion of what ought to be done, and the entire absence of subsequent compulsion in
the doing of it. When the force of the
moral imperative is felt most absolutely,
the hand of external necessity is withdrawn, that we may act freely. Consciously
hemmed in and weighed down by physical forces within the sphere of Nature, —
forces which we are powerless to resist,
— the pressure is relaxed, within the moral
sphere; and we are free to go to the right
hand or to the left, when duty appeals to
us on the one side, and desire on the other.
This has been so excellently put by Mr.
Richard Hutton, in his essay on "the
Atheistic Explanation of Religion," that I
may quote a sentence, which sums up the
ethical argument for the Divine Personal-

ity, better than any other that I am aware
of : —

Accustomed as man is to feel his personal feebleness,
his entire subordination to the physical forces of the
universe, . . . in the case of moral duty he finds this
almost constant pressure remarkably withdrawn at the
very crisis in which the import of his actions is brought
home to him with the most vivid conviction. Of what
nature can a power be that moves us hither and thither
through the ordinary course of our lives, but withdraws
its hands at those critical points where we have the
clearest sense of authority, in order to let us act for ourselves? The absolute control that sways so much of
our life is waived just where we are impressed with the
most profound conviction that there is but one path in
which we can move with a free heart. If so, are we not
then surely *watched?* Is it not clear that the Power
which has therein ceased to *move* us has retired only to
observe? . . . The mind is pursued into its freest movements by this belief that the Power within could only
voluntarily have receded from its task of moulding us,
in order to keep watch over us, as we mould ourselves.[1]

It is thus that the dualism, involved in
all knowledge, comes out in sharpest prominence in the moral sphere. There we rise
at once, above the uniformity of mere phe-
nomenalism, and out of the thralldom of
necessity, by recognizing the transcendent
element that is latent in the conscience.
We escape from the circle of self altogether, in the "otherness" of moral law.

[1] *Essays, Theological and Literary*, vol. i. pp. 41, 42.

It is in the ethical field that we meet with the most significant facts, which prevent us from gliding, through a seductive love of unity, into a pantheistic solution of the problem of existence. The fascination of the pursuit of unity, through all the diversities of finite exi..tence, has given rise to many philosophical systems, which have twisted the facts of consciousness to one side. But unity is by itself as unintelligible, as diversity minus unity is unthinkable. If there were but one self-existing Substance, of which all individual forms of being were tributary streams, the relation of any single rill to its source (and to the whole) would be merely that of derivation. Moral ties would be lost, in a union that was purely physical. On this theory, the universe would be one, only because there was nothing in it to unite; whereas all moral unity implies diversity, and is based upon it. There must be a difference in the things which are connected by an underlying and under-working affinity. And we find this difference most apparent in the phenomena of the moral cosnciousness. While, therefore, the moral law legislates, and desire opposes, in the struggle that ensues between inclination and duty, we trace the working of a principle, which has not grown out of our desires and their gratification. We discover that we are not, like the links in the chain of physical nature, passive instruments for the development of the increasing purpose of things; but that we exist for the unfolding, disciplining, and completing of a life of self-control, and the inward mastery of impulse, through which, at the great crises of moral decision, a new world of experience is entered.

We cannot tell when this began. Its origin is lost in the golden haze that is wrapped around our infancy, when personal life is not consciously distinguishable from automatic action. But as our faculties enlarge, a point is reached when the individual perceives the significance of freedom, the meaning of the august rules of righteousness, and the grave issues of voluntary choice. It is then that conscience

> Gives out at times
> A little flash, a mystic hint

of a Personality distinct from ours, yet kindred to it, in the unity of which it lives, and has its being. Whence come those suggestions of the Infinite — that flit athwart the stage of consciousness, in our struggle and aspiration after the ideal — if not from a Personal Source kindred to themselves? We do not create our own longings in this direction. On the contrary, as we advance from infancy to maturity, we come, by slow progressive steps, to the knowledge of a vast over-shadowing Personality, — unseen yet supra-sensible, recognized at intervals then lost to view, known and unknown, — surrounding, enfolding, inspiring, and appealing to us, in the suggestions of the moral faculty? In addition to this, our sense of the boundlessness of duty brings with it a suggestion of the infinity of its Source. We know it to be beyond ourselves, and higher than we, extra-human; even extra-mundane; while, on other grounds, we know it to be also intra-human and intra-mundane. We find no difficulty in realizing that the Personality, revealed to us in conscience, may have infinite relations and affinities; because, in no district of the universe, can we conceive the verdict of the moral law reversed. Nowhere would

it be right not "to do justly, and to love
mercy," although the practical rules and
minor canons of morality may, like cere-
monial codes, change with the place in
which they originate, and the circumstances
which gave rise to them. If, therefore,
the suffrage of the race has not created
this inward monitor, and if its sway is co-
extensive with the sphere of moral agency,
— if its range is as vast as its authority is
absolute — in these facts we have corroborative evidence of the union of the Personal with the Infinite.

IMMORTALITY.

In discussing this large subject, which periodically comes to the front, and occupies, if it does not agitate, every thoughtful mind, — the question, viz., of the survival of the individual when this life ends, — it is above all things necessary to keep within the lines of verifiable evidence, in order that we may lean on no broken, and, if possible, on no breakable reed. It is also necessary to distinguish between what we actually know, and what we merely surmise, or may legitimately hope for. If it is not likely (as I do not think it is) that many new proofs will be forthcoming, — proofs that will set the question finally at rest, — it is desirable that all the old ones should be recast, from age to age. Still more important is it that the great mass of inconclusive argument, which so easily accumulates on a subject of such importance, should be cleared away, in order that we may see where the foundation stones are lying.

Many persons seem to me to desiderate
far more, in the way of positive evidence
on this subject, than it is desirable *à priori*
to expect, or than the experience of the
past warrants us in hoping to obtain.   One
distinguished writer has told us, sorrow-
fully, that he has found " no logical reasons
to compel conviction."   But he forgets
that, if such existed, the controversy would
be closed.   If there was no possibility of
questioning the doctrine, in its very obviousness it would be shorn of half its grandeur.   It would sink to the level of a secondary truth, if not to the lower level of a
commonplace conviction.   It is sometimes
forgotten that all perfectly luminous truths
are secondary ones.   Truths that are primary, or ultimate, are of necessity dim ;
because, whenever we pass beyond phenomena, the reality which we apprehend is
half concealed, as well as half revealed.
In our more impatient and shallow moods
we may wish it were otherwise ; but, in all
the profounder moments of experience, we
do not desire that these ultimate convictions should be lowered to the level of the
perfectly obvious.   It will be seen that several important moral ends are served by

the very obscurity of the problem with which we are to deal.

It is expedient, first, of all to set aside the irrelevant arguments that have been advanced, both in favor of the doctrine and against it; always remembering that, as every error is a truth abused, many a faulty argument may spring from a root existing somewhere in human nature, or beyond it; and that, with all its irrelevancy or inconclusiveness, it may be merely the distortion of a truth, which only requires to be reset, in order to afford valid corroborative testimony.

I put aside the instinctive desire or longing for continued life, because we desire and long for many things which we cannot possibly get. We may note, however, that it is not on the mere wish for immortality that the argument is based, but rather on this, that, since the stream of instinctive tendency sets in that direction so strongly, some real magnet, and no mere illusion, must be drawing it forth. Thus, the desire may be prophetic of its own fulfillment. We may take the statement of Aquinas as an embodiment of this argument, "Naturale desiderium non potest esse inane ;" but the inference is invalid, and must be set aside unhesitatingly. We set aside also the proof drawn from the consent of the ages. In reference to immortality there is no *consensus gentium.* It is not in the category of the "quod semper, quod ubique, quod ab omnibus." Then, there is the argument from analogy. There is no analogy, however, between any phenomenal change in the physical world and that which supervenes when soul and body separate. The doctrine of immortality is thus outwith or beyond experience. It has been said that as the worm changes into the chrysalis, and the chrysalis into the fly, while both are in a rudimentary manner within the worm from the first, our act of dying may be merely "the shuffling off " of " a mortal coil " which liberates the spirit. But there is no analogy between the two. The only valid parallel would be the immediate appearance of another *body ;* as, when a crustacean casts its shell, the new one already exists within that which is thrown aside. The butterfly is materially within the caterpillar ; and the vital principle does not desert the worm or the crustacean, and appear detached from its old envelope. It only slumbers in the one, and reawakens in the other. Thus no physical consideration is of any value in favor of the survival of the human soul. Grant that matter cannot by itself fashion the material molecules into the shapes which they assume, and that this is due to an immaterial principle working in and through it, it does not follow that the vital force which accretes these molecules and vitalizes them must continue to live, independently of the work it does.

But now, with these arguments candidly laid aside, there are others, constantly advanced against immortality, which must be set aside as equally baseless. By far the strongest of these is the present dependence of the human soul upon the body; the correlation of the two being so close, that the vigor of the one waxes and wanes with the vigor of the other. So far as experience guides us, this dependence is constant, though not absolute; and it is inferred that, being inseparable now, when the one dies the other must perish with it. This, however, is an illegitimate inference. The present correlation of mind and matter, in the conscious life of soul and body,

can prove nothing against the immortality
of the former ; and if, during the present
life, our vital phenomena are only *the sensible signs of a reality beyond themselves,*
their cessation as phenomena is not necessarily the cessation of life itself. We may
note further that, while analogy is incompetent to prove immortality, it is equally
incapable of disproving it, and that it cannot, in the least degree, discredit it. It
does not follow that, because the elements
out of which the body is composed are
refunded to nature on the death of the
organism, the same must take place with
regard to the soul, unless we can prove,
on independent grounds, that mind is but
a function of body, when of course the
function would cease with the cessation
of its organ.

I have now to refer to certain arguments, lying midway between those already mentioned, and the more valid ones
to which we afterwards proceed. These
intermediate proofs are founded on an alleged necessity for the completion or full
development of powers, for which the present life gives no adequate scope. They
may be called psychological arguments, be-

cause they arise out of the contrast between the results attained in this life and the possibilities of attainment. In the case of lower organisms, this does not hold good. They perish by the thousand, incomplete; they are nipped in the bud by the million. But the argument, — or rather the suggestion, or "intimation of immortality," — in the case of man, may be put thus. The total absence of completion within terrestrial limits, as compared with the approximate realization of it, in the case of the lower creatures within these limits, suggests for man a sphere and an arena in the future in which completion will be possible. In the case of the flower, the insect, and the tree, there is a fixed limit of development. Further growth is impossible. So with man's body; beyond a definite though variable limit it cannot possibly continue to exist. Its functions wear out. The human consciousness, on the other hand, never blossoms into perfect form within the limits of the "threescore years and ten." Of course the physiologist will tell us that the two must develop together, and that the one cannot continue when the other ends. The rejoinder, however,

is obvious : in autumn, the flower *must*
fade, because it has done its work. Not
only do external climatic conditions compel decay, the internal state of the organism necessitates it. But this cannot
be affirmed with the same confidence, or
on the same grounds, of the human soul.
We have no evidence that, when the limits
of the bodily organism are reached, the
mental and moral faculties have attained
their goal. On the contrary, they *often
seem to be just commencing their development.* This is especially seen on the moral
side of experience, in reference to the capacities of human virtue and affection.
Their utterly inadequate development in
this life, as compared with their possibilities of expansion, and still more their latent conscious affinities, suggests a future
in which there will be room for enlargement. The mere existence of those moral
ideals — which expand as we approach towards them, and which recede perpetually
before the inward eye that contemplates
them — suggests, not the fugitive chase of
a phantom, the pursuit of a will-o'-the-wisp,
but a future emancipation from fetters
which now arrest the development of energy.

Before I state the grounds on which —
in the absence of any evidence against immortality — our moral intuitions (and such
suggestions as those just referred to) may
be allowed to come in, and to weight the
scale of probability in its favor, a remark
may be made on the scorn with which the
latter kind of evidence is received in certain quarters.   Perhaps it is not every mind
that can admit the force of the evidence of
intuition — which is a sort of divination, or
purified second-sight, kindred to the poet's
vision of the universe; but it is worthy of
note that, as it bears upon the future, this
intuition is invariably keenest in the best
of men.   It is the noblest characters whose
attainments in virtue and goodness are
greatest, those who have done most for
their fellow-men, in whom this presage of
the future is most vivid; and, further, it is
in their loftiest moments that the conjecture is keenest.   It is the surmise of the
highest element in human nature.

> The wish that of the living whole,
> No life should fail beyond the grave,
> Derives it not from what we hold,
> The likest God within the soul?

This surmise often intensifies, toward the

close of life. Some of the best of men, as they have approached the inevitable barrier, have had the clearest sight of what lies beyond it. And the poets — as Tennyson, in his "Crossing the Bar," and Browning in his final "Reverie" — have spoken on the subject in their old age with a clearer voice of prophecy.

But the answer which we give to the problem of immortality must depend on how we answer a prior question. That prior question relates to the soul's nature and inherent characteristics. If we have good grounds for believing that we are more than a succession of states of changing experience, if a thread of personality and of inner continuity runs through all that we are, — so that we are not mere functions of organization, — we may have good grounds for believing that the body *does not possess us*, so to speak, but *that we possess it*, and that we are therefore separate and separable from it. Here we must fall back on the testimony of consciousness ; and while no one can do this vicariously, or by proxy for another, I think that the following will be found to be a fact which awaits discovery, and which has

only to be sought in order to be found, viz.,
that while, during the present life, we are
gradually gathering together a mass of experience of all sorts, we are, or we may be,
conscious all the time of an underlying self
as a centre round which this experience
gathers. We are continuously conscious
of the mind's dependence upon the body,
but it does not follow that this dependence
destroys its independence. We know that,
if the brain is injured, the manifestations
of thought are impaired, and that if the
brain is destroyed the manifestations of
thought cease; but it does not follow that
thought itself ceases, or that the conscious
life of the mind comes to an end.

I admit that the array of statistics by
which the dependence of mind on brain is
established is the most formidable fact, or
series of facts, with which the spiritualist
has to deal in this inquiry. But surely it
is an equally arresting fact in our conscious experience that the mind's present
relation to the body is that of dependence
and independence combined. I deny that
it is wholly dependent, or that it is entirely
independent; I affirm it to be both the one
and the other. At certain times the de-

pendence may be at a maximum, and the independence at a minimum; but at other times it is precisely the reverse. In moments of heightened consciousness every one knows how energy rises and asserts itself, sometimes even chafing with the trammels of the physical organism. We cannot, of course, be conscious of the detachment of the mind from the body; but we are habitually conscious of an inward energy, which rises and falls within us, alternately dominating over the organism and succumbing to it, and which, therefore, may be finally separable from it. Then is it not an undoubted fact that the operations of mind are more perfect, the freer they are from the restraints of the body? Up to a certain normal point the body aids the mind; beyond that point it tyrannizes over it. Take this fact in connection with the frequent consciousness of powers possessed but unused, of powers locked up, or held down by the fetters of the flesh, latent energies, which are now in us in a state similar to that in which our senses were in the embryonic stage. Does not this suggest the mind's independence of its organism? Grant that, with all those heightenings and brightenings of consciousness, there is — as the physiologists remind us — a definite coördination of molecular states, the former are at least simultaneous suggestions of the inner freedom of the spirit. They suggest that it is not the slave of the body in which it is lodged, but rather in the position of a temporary tenant. If, then, our personality is not due to the body, may it not survive when the body falls to pieces? Wherein lies the difficulty of supposing that the individual carries within him the seeds of immortality, which cannot ripen where they are at present, but which — like the mummy wheat in Egyptian tombs — may supply the harvests of the future?

The whole controversy hinges on the question of the origin of mind, and whether molecular motion can give rise to human consciousness. That it can, is the materialistic thesis; that it cannot, is the spiritualistic antithesis. The materialistic thesis is, I maintain, unverifiable; because (1) no amount of research amongst external phenomena can touch the question of the source of those phenomena of which we are conscious, or bring us within sight of its solution; and (2) if there be an interior principle which binds together the isolated threads of thought and feeling, we have direct evidence that our personality is not due to a mere passive evolution, but that it is the product of an active power working within phenomena, arranging and coördinating them. If, therefore, we are more than phenomena, we may at least surmise that we do not perish and pass away, as phenomena do.

There is no doubt that, so far as the evidence of *sense* can guide us, death is the end of the individual. Nothing can follow but a rearrangement of the molecules of matter, in some new individual form, or in one without individuality. No one doubts that the quantity of matter within the universe neither increases nor diminishes. It only changes. It appears for a time vitalized, but its vitality is only *for a time.* The question is, What becomes of the vital principle, when it ceases to animate a certain group of atoms? Does it simply fall back into the great reservoir of cosmic force, out of which it came, like a stream returning to the sea in which it is lost; or does its individual-

ity survive, detached from the old form
that now has perished, but still retaining
power to build up around it a fresh group
of atoms, a new phenomenal abode in a future state of existence?

When we strive to answer the question
just stated, there is one important fact
which may help our conjectures, viz., this:
that the vital force which at present constitutes our personality, and builds it up,
is perpetually changing. Not for two moments of time is the arrangement of the
molecules of matter within any living organism the same; nor is the coexistence
of thought and feeling stationary for a single instant within the mind of any individual. Our present life is a dynamical
process of incessant change, of progressive
evolution and development; but throughout this whole process, our individuality
survives. Individuality is not only consistent with change, but change is absolutely necessary to it. It is essential to
the very life of the individual. Why, then,
may not the individuality of the individual
continue after the larger and more thor-
oughgoing change of the molecules which
we call death?

Add to this that we have no evidence whatsoever that the mental phenomena of the present life are the mere functions of organization. We might quite as well, or with equal justice, affirm that material phenomena were mere phases of mind. All that we discover in experience is that thoughts and feelings are associated with physical states, and *vice versâ*. They are corelated and coördinated, how we do not know. Are we not at liberty to infer that, if mental phenomena are not produced by physical ones, they are not tied to them, but are detachable from them? It is true that we find our mental states heightened by their physical accessories, but our physical states are as certainly influenced by mental ones. Action and reaction between them is reciprocal and complementary. What is the inference from their present conjunction? Not that the one of necessity ceases when the other does, but that they are temporary allies, coöperating now, but capable of new affinities, of fresh groupings, and developments in another sphere of existence.

I shall now mention, without enlarging on them, the more significant facts belonging to our *moral* nature which suggest the immortality of the individual.

There is, first, the intrinsic character of moral life, as compared with mere physical vitality. It is said that moral life carries with it the evidence of indestructibility, because there is nothing in human love, reverence, or devotion, that is naturally perishable. There is nothing exclusively terrestrial in friendship. It is outreaching and transcendent, in its inner essence amaranthine; but, if all is over, when — to human vision — life ends at death, the question, "To what purpose is this waste?" would be the most pertinent of inquiries. This argument, or suggestion, becomes stronger, if taken in connection with the teleological explanation of the universe, as a sphere in which purpose is visible, a system of natural means working towards natural ends. Here is an apparatus within the cosmic order, — namely, our human life, — constructed with an outreaching or prospective element in it. Is not this arrangement, this structure, to be interpreted by us as prophetic of the future?

Secondly, a future is needed for the completion of what is undeveloped here and now, for the maturing of what at present finds no scope for expansion, and no arena in which to work. As one, to whom the poetic "intimations of immortality" were specially vivid, has elsewhere written,

> Too, too contracted are these walls of flesh,
> This vital warmth too cold, these visual orbs,
> Though inconceivably endowed, too dim
> For any passion of the soul that leads
> To ecstasy, and all the crooked paths
> Of time and change disdaining, takes its course
> Along the line of limitless desires.

Thirdly, it is said that a future is needed for the rectification of those moral anomalies which are inexplicable without it, and which at present seem rather to suggest a dualistic than a monotheistic theory of the universe. Reward and punishment are not now measured out in proportion to the desert of individuals; therefore it is inferred that the present life is but the prelude to another, in which justice will be done. This fact, — which runs through all history, and is the secret of all tragedy, — viz., that the innocent often suffer when the guilty escape, suggests, in the words of Jouffroy, that "human life is a drama, of which the prologue and the catastrophe are both wanting."

The argument may be altered thus. It is clear that in this life all men do not reap as they sow. Some sow to the flesh, and have the best of it ; others sow to the spirit, and have the worst of it — *so far as the present life is concerned.* If, therefore, it is part of the general stream of tendency that the outward and inward should ultimately harmonize — that virtue and happiness should form a true moral equation — since they do not now run on parallel lines, is not a future state necessary for rectification ? If we live in a world over which a great Moral Order dominates, and in which the laws of conduct are supreme, we certainly also live in one in which these laws are at present, in the vast majority of instances, broken down and overthrown. In other words, the arrangements of the universe *de facto* are not what they ought to be *de jure*. This therefore either suggests a future in which there will be a readjustment, or it suggests the Zoroastrian doctrine of a conflict between the powers of light and darkness, Ormuzd and Ahriman, good and evil, in eternal strife.

These moral considerations are not ab-

solute proofs, any more than the previous
ones. They are presumptions, which ripen
into likelihoods ; and they are certainly
sufficient to weight the scale on the side
of immortality, as against the opposite doctrine.

It is quite as important, however, to note
some of the effects of the presence and the
absence of a belief in immortality on human conduct, as it is to gather evidence
in its favor, because these effects may be
turned into evidence.   Let it be granted
that on the theory that the existence
of the individual terminates at death, the
moral value of the present life is not destroyed ; and, further, that the anticipation
of immortality does not usually become a
motive to well-doing, "in the case of those
who would not be virtuous without it."
Most pernicious teaching has sometimes
been put forth on this subject, by those
who have affirmed that all morality hinges
on a belief in immortality.   This is simply
untrue to fact.   Belief in a spiritual Order,
and in a moral Standard, has coexisted
(whether logically or not) with belief in
the annihilation of man ; but I agree with
a distinguished American writer on the

subject, who says "that the effect of the rejection of the belief is to give the great motor nerve of our moral life a perceptible stroke of palsy," and that the moral value of the belief lies in these three things: the light which it casts on the otherwise bewildering mysteries of the present, the motive it supplies for noble action, and the solace which it yields under overwhelming disaster. It is quite true that our duty does not depend upon the length of our days, but upon our existing relations; but if these relations are contracted within the horizon of the present, an arrest is laid upon some of our noblest aspirations; and, contrariwise, where the belief in immortality is present, and regulative, duty is seen under a fresh light, its scope is widened, its significance enlarged, and its pursuit made easier.

It is one of the most curious things, however, in the history of opinion, that this belief in immortality has been assailed as hostile to morality, as egotistic and vain, as a selfish idea which develops selfishness in those who cherish it. It has been represented as the outcome of mere conceit that any one should fancy himself an exception to the universal law that whatsoever appears in time must in time disappear. It is further affirmed that human virtue moves most securely within terrestrial limits, and that the forecastings of the future which this belief engenders break in upon and mar

> The sober majesties
> Of settled sweet epicurean life.

The prospect of the future darkens our present existence, it is said, by its shadow, or its menace.

Now such a result is only possible where the doctrine of immortality has been either travestied or caricatured. It is the way in which a belief is cherished that makes its effect either selfish or the reverse, and there have been both very humble and very proud believers in immortality, just as there have been both humble and proud believers in annihilation.

As to the influence of the belief on conduct, the most important question is not, does this or that individual hold the doctrine? but does the doctrine hold them? *i. e.*, does it dominate their thoughts, and exert a controlling influence on conduct?

Now the doctrine of annihilation, as

taught in the materialistic and agnostic schools, has undoubtedly given rise — and is much more likely than its opposite to give rise — to selfishness, and indifference to other lives and interests. That a belief in the existence of an infinite Moral Source whence the laws of conduct emanate, and in the continued existence of finite moral natures by whom these laws are exemplified, should lessen their authority *now*, may be set down with perfect charity as a speculative paradox, a vagary, or an intellectual whim. The contrary supposition that they are the mere outcome of cosmic forces — blind, relentless, and stern — which may go on developing and evolving others different from them, might possibly lower, and often has lowered, their authority; but the belief that they are the finite reflection of an infinite Reality, and that there is a supreme Consciousness overshadowing us, and answering to our limited apprehension of moral truth, has always given force and point, as well as elevation, to present duty.

The blank which is left in human life, if this belief be removed from it, is further seen, when we consider the substitutes proposed to be put in its place ; such, for example, as the immortality of influence, the indestructibility of our deeds, which live on forever in their consequences, *post mortem corporis.* Now, in the first place, the offer of this as a substitute shows that the human heart cannot surrender its belief in immortality without some compensation. But, in the second place, to accept it as an equivalent is to accept a stone instead of bread. It is no substitute at all, because the immortality of influence is common to all theories on the subject. It is no compensation to one about to be deprived of a possession for the spoiler to say, " Well ; you may keep the half of it," though it may be a slight mitigation of the loss. And, thirdly, the unsatisfactoriness of what remains — this posthumous influence — is apparent when one realizes the mixed character of all that is transmitted by us. It is unhappily true that " the evil that men do lives after them, the good is oft interred with their bones ; " and if the thought of how our deeds will tell upon our successors be the sole motive left to animate us to noble or disinterested action, I fear it will become more and more attenuated and vague. It is too shadowy and remote to influence any but a select few. The masses of mankind, "the dim common populations," cannot take it in.

Then there is the doctrine, which was Spinoza's substitute for the immortality of the individual, viz., that we have nothing to do with duration in time, because in our knowledge of the Infinite we transcend time, and are now immortal, in the only sense in which it is worth thinking of immortality, — immortal, that is to say, in virtue of our escape from the world of illusions, and our seeing all things *sub specie æternitatis.* Spinoza thought that to speak of immortality as a thing of the future was to destroy its very nature, because if we merely think of an extension of duration we are still in thralldom to time, and are not therefore really immortal; and that we attain to immortality, now and here, simply by rising into the higher sphere of thought, in which we contemplate the universe as everlasting. But however true this may be in one sense, in another it is altogether misleading. It ignores our relation to the phenomenal world, and if we discard the notion of immortality in time, it will be easy for the opponents of the doctrine to claim us as on their side. It will be said, What is the value of an immortality that does not last? Is it not a contradiction in terms? Spinoza's view of immortality is not the continuous existence of mind after the body dies, but merely the capacity in the present life to rise above time, and see all things under the form of eternity. He thought that to look onward to our survival in time was to explain by means of the temporal what in its essence transcended time; and so, the mere notion of eternity — into which the mind enters when disillusioned by philosophy — was sufficient without any further idea of continuance or lastingness. But if this latter element, which is all in all to the opposite philosophy, be discarded, the present life is not explained; and if this intuition of the Infinite, which may be reached by any of us in time, passes away, if it vanishes for us when we disappear from the earth, what is its value? If it begins and ends for us with our terrestrial lives, may it not be surmised to have a material origin altogether?

On these substitutes for the survival of

the individual I need not enlarge, but may now point out some of the results which follow from a rejection of the doctrine.

We cannot prove a belief to be erroneous by merely tracing out its consequences; but the discovery of startling practical results, issuing inevitably from the adoption of a given theory, may suggest the likelihood of a flaw somewhere about the root of that theory. Taking, then, past experience as our guide, we may affirm that, whenever this belief has for a time disappeared, or fallen away from the foreground of consciousness, there has been a simultaneous decline in the nobler elements of civilization — in Poetry, in Art, in Philosophy, and even in Science. More particularly, the affections of human nature have suffered; their tenderness and delicacy have been blunted. If they are but mundane ties, by which human beings are associated together for a time, but which are snapped finally at death, even their temporal significance is lessened. Duty becomes an affair of custom, of fashion, and of temperament. Morality, as we have said, does not hinge upon the belief in immortality; but the motives for self-control and self-discipline

are *changed*, if we may legitimately surmise that we have been evolved out of the
material universe, in the slow progression
of the ages, and that it is our destiny to
return to the abyss when this life ends.
It is easy to see how different is the effect
of a belief that, in the hints and suggestions of the moral faculty, we are acted
upon by an infinite Intelligence and an infinite Personality, and that our relation to
that infinitely intelligent Personality is not
limited to the present life, but survives beyond it. The conviction that we not only
now live and move within the Infinite, and
yet are distinct from it, *but that we shall
always do so*, has a direct and immediate
influence, and an " uplifting influence," on
conduct. With this conviction removed,
human friendship degenerates to the level
of casual acquaintanceship, as with the
herds of " dumb driven cattle ; " and moral
life, with its sublime struggles towards
a distant goal, shrivels into commonplace,
while it contracts within the limits of the
secular. What is the consequence ? The
majority of men will say, *cui bono ?* What
boots it, all this toil to reach a higher life,
if, at the end of it, we sink into the jaws of

darkness, and cease to be? "Let us eat and drink, for to-morrow we die."

Before indicating what seems to be the wisest attitude of mind towards this problem, we may note some of the causes which have led many of our contemporaries to throw it into the background of conviction, rather than bring it to the forefront. There is, first, the speculative mystery into which the belief runs up. There is, next, the necessary absence of any experimental evidence in regard to it. Again, there is the difficulty of granting immortality to man, and denying it to the higher animals that resemble him in many ways; and the impossibility of granting the latter, and stopping short at any point in the chain of organized life. Further, there is the natural recoil which many feel from the over-dogmatic confidence with which the future has been spoken of, and the gross material conceptions which have been entertained of it; and also an equally natural recoil from the asceticism that undervalues the present life, because of the tremendousness of its sequel. These are natural reactions. Then, there is the absorption of mind and of interest in things material, which is so marked a feature of our age, the stream of tendency setting strongly towards a physical explanation of spiritual phenomena. Further, there is a feeling of life-weariness, of the burden of existence after a time, and with this the inclination to lay it down, to escape from the present turmoil by an absorption like that of Nirvana, — the feeling that, if finally we sleep, we shall do well. The loss of faith in the future which arises from this feeling of life-weariness, accompanied by a loss of interest in life itself, has some-times spread through a whole community, or historic period; but it does not last. At least it does not last with us in the West. It is more an Eastern than a Western tendency, due perhaps to mental, moral, and physical causes combined.

Another phase of the difficulty at times oppresses most men in the West, as well as the Orientals; and there are moods of mind in which it appeals to all who think deeply and reverently on the subject. Doubt as to immortality may be due to humility. It may spring from a sense of the poverty of our faculties, and the tremendous enigma which the problem —

when all has been said about it — presents to them. I have mentioned some features of that enigma. Here is another aspect of it. We can watch the beginnings of life on this earth, we know how the generations succeed each other by a process of development, in reference to which experience is our guide; but we have no similar evidence of the survival of any single creature after its life on earth has been cut short by death.

Perhaps the chief question is not whether we are to survive? but in what form is the survival to be experienced? What *kind* of immortality is to be ours? *What* is it to be, and *where* is it to be? Will we survive with our present identity, our moral individuality, retained? and will we, in the next stage, be conscious of the relations we have sustained to this life as it now is? On these points, we have very little light. Doubtless, unless we retained an individuality of some sort, it would not be *we* who survived. But, on the other hand, is there not a very great deal about this present life that is of necessity transient? and are there not many things that we fain would lose? Very few desire to remain what they are, and as they are. Perhaps the absolute loss of a large part of present experience would be to the majority of us a positive gain; and yet, unless we who have played our part on the stage of this life continue, with rememberable ties connecting us with it, and possessed of affinities that remain unchanged though enlarged, how can immortality in any sense be ours?

The whole problem is beset with difficulties, both on the right hand and on the left. Our truest and wisest attitude toward it is one of tranquil hope and devout expectancy, tempered by cheerful acquiescence; while we hail any further light that may be vouchsafed to others, through the happy auguries of a reverent outlook. This mood of mind has been well expressed in one of Wordsworth's sonnets, in which he likens our present life to that of a bird that has entered a lighted room from the outside darkness and cold, that flutters within it for a while, and then departs.

Man's life is like a Sparrow, mighty King!
That — while at banquet with your chiefs you sit
Housed near a blazing fire, — is seen to flit
Safe from the wintry tempest. Fluttering,

Here did it enter ; there, on hasty wing
Flies out, and passes on from cold to cold ;
But whence it came we know not, nor behold
Whither it goes.   Even such that transient Thing,
The human Soul ; not utterly unknown
While in the Body lodged, her warm abode ;
But from what world She came, what woe or weal
On her departure waits, no tongue hath shown ;
This mystery if the Stranger can reveal,
His be a welcome cordially bestowed.

THE DOCTRINE OF METEMPSY-
CHOSIS.

I⊤ seems surprising that in the discussions of contemporary philosophy on the origin and destiny of the soul, there has been no explicit revival of the doctrines of Preëxistence and Metempsychosis. Whatever may be their intrinsic worth, or evidential value, their title to rank on the roll of philosophical hypotheses is undoubted. They offer quite as remarkable a solution of the mystery which all admit as the rival theories of Creation, Traduction, and Extinction.

What I propose is not so much to defend the doctrines, as to restate them; to distinguish between their several forms; to indicate the speculative grounds on which the most rational of them may be maintained; to show how it fits as well into a theistic as into a pantheistic theory of the universe; and to point out the difficulties in the ethical problem which it lightens if it does not remove.

The question may be best approached by a statement of the chief difficulty which seems to block the way to a belief in Immortality, — arising out of the almost universal acceptance of the doctrine of Evolution as explanatory of physical existence, — and one of the considerations by which it has been met. This will lead, by natural sequence, to the theories in question.

The difficulty is this. Admitting the development of man out of prior conditions, and retaining a belief in his immortality, a point must have been reached when a mortal predecessor gave rise to an immortal successor. If all that now is has issued inexorably out of what once was, and the human race been gradually evolved out of a prior type, we have but three alternatives to choose from: either, first, the whole series is mortal ; or, second, the whole is immortal ; or, third, a long series of mortal ancestors gave place, at a leap and a bound, to an immortal descendant, the father of a race of immortals. There is no other possible alternative, if we admit a process of development. The first of the three may be set aside meanwhile, since it is the doctrine of the natural mortality or extinction

of the individual. The second presents the
insuperable difficulty of the continued existence in a separate form of all the living
creatures that have ever appeared on the
stage of being ; because it is impossible to
draw a line anywhere amongst them, and
say that the dog is immortal but the reptile
is not ; or that the reptile is, while the bee
and the ant are not ; or that they are, while
the myriad tribes of the protozoa are not.
We are, therefore, limited to the third hypothesis, viz., that a point was reached
when immortality was evolved ; that is to
say, that the power of surviving the shock
of dissolution was non-existent for ages, but
that it became real in a moment of time,
when the mortal creature that preceded
man gave birth to one who was an " heir
of immortality." In stating the problem
thus, I merely indicate the logical result of
admitting the principle of Evolution as explanatory of physical existence, and con-
joining with it the doctrine of Immortality.
The derivation of the human body from
a lower type is quite consistent with the
latter doctrine, because the body is not
immortal. It is, besides, a much worthier
notion, and more in keeping with analogy,

to suppose that the body was formed by natural process out of a previous animal organization, than to imagine it to have been instantaneously created out of the inorganic dust of the world. But was the human soul similarly evolved out of the vital principal of the previous races? Was the ζωή of the animal the parent of the ψυχή. or πνεῦμα, in man? If we answer in the affirmative we adopt the development theory in its completest form; and it is certain that man cannot be immortal. His race may be permanent (although, by the hypothesis, it is perpetually altering), but the individuals composing it cannot live forever. It is impossible, in short, that Immortality can be a prerogative evolved out of mortality, because the one is separated from the other, to use an expressive phrase of Norris's, " by the whole diameter of being." This is the difficulty in question.

It has been met, or attempted to be met, by the following consideration. It is alleged that the case was precisely the same in reference to the first immortal evolved out of a mortal ancestor, as it is in reference to any of his descendants; because, in both cases, the beginnings of life are

similar. These may be physiologically
traced ; and a point is always reached when
a possible mortality is averted. The "first
beginnings of individual life," says Mr.
Picton, "do not involve immortality : and
when such an incipient merely germinant
life deceases, it perishes utterly." There
must be a period reached, therefore, at
which immortality begins. " If an individual died one moment before a certain time
he would be annihilated : whereas, if he
survives a moment longer, he will live forever."[1]   And so it is thought that a time
comes when the personality of the individual matures, when " his isolation grows
defined," and he is thenceforward able to
"survive the shock of death ; " whereas,
had his bodily organization perished one
moment earlier, his destiny would have
been simply to remerge in the general
whole. Thus, the immaterial principle,
which in a thousand cases dies and passes
into some other form of immaterial energy,
survives in the case of others, and wins
permanence for itself by successfully re-
sisting the first perils of independent life.
Such is the rejoinder.

[1] *New Theories and the Old Faith*, p. 199.

I cannot think this way of escaping the difficulty a satisfactory one, unless the principle which survives is believed to have existed previously in some other form. The difference between immortality and mortality is not one of degree. It is literally infinite, and the one can never give rise to the other. The immortal cannot, in the nature of things, be developed out of the mortal. A creature endowed with feeble powers of life may originate another endowed with stronger powers, which will therefore live longer, and be able to survive the storms which have shipwrecked its feebler ancestors; but this is a totally different thing from the evolution of an immortal progeny out of a series of mortal predecessors. Let us suppose, however, that the immortal has descended, that it has " lapsed from higher place," or that it has ascended, risen from some lower sphere, immortality may then *belong to its very essence.* It may, in its inmost nature, be incapable of death, its destiny being a perpetual transmigration, or renewal of existence. The distinction between a theory of evolution (which admits immortality) and that of transmigration is immense. According to the former, man at a definite moment of time emerged out of the animal, and the power of surviving the shock of death was conferred upon him, or won by him, in the struggle for existence. According to the latter, man was always immortal ; before he entered the present life he existed in another state, and he will survive the destruction of his present body simply because his soul, which is intrinsically deathless, passes into a new body, or remains temporarily unembodied. The difference is immense. On the other hand, the distinction between the theory of transmigration and that of absorption is equally great. According to the one, the soul retains its individuality and preserves its identity through all the changes it undergoes ; according to the other, its individuality is lost, although its vital force ′survives as an ineradicable constituent of the universe.

The doctrine of Metempsychosis is theoretically extremely simple. Its root is the indestructibility of the vital principle. Let a belief in preëxistence be joined to that of posthumous existence, and the dogma is complete. It is thus at one and the same time a theory of the soul's origin, and of its destination ; and its unparalleled hold upon the human race may be explained in part by the fact of its combining both in a single doctrine. It appears as one of the very earliest beliefs of the human mind in tribes not emerged from barbarism. It remains the creed of millions at this day. It is probably the most widely-spread and permanently influential of all speculative theories as to the origin and destiny of the soul.

In a single paragraph its history may be sketched, though in the most condensed and cursory manner. It has lain at the heart of all Indian speculation on the subject, time out of mind. It is one of the cardinal doctrines of the Vedas, and one of the roots of Buddhist belief. The ancient Egyptians held it. It is prominent in their great classic, the "Book of the Dead." In Persia, it colored the whole stream of Zoroastrian thought. The Magi taught it. The Jews brought it with them from the captivity in Babylon. Many of the Essenes and Pharisees held it. Though foreign to the genius both of Judaism and Christianity, it has had its advocates (as Delitzsch puts it) "as well in the synagogue as in the church." The Cabbala teaches it emphatically. The Apocrypha sanctions it, and it is to be found scattered throughout the Talmud. In Greece, Pythagoras proclaimed it, receiving the hint probably both from Egypt and the East; Empedocles taught it; Plato worked it elaborately out, not as a mythical doctrine embodying a moral truth, but as a philosophical theory or conviction. It passed over into the Neo-Platonic School at Alexandria. Philo held it. Plotinus and Porphyry in the third century, Jamblicus in the fourth, Hierocles and Proclus in the fifth, all advocated it in various ways; and an important modification of the Platonic doctrine took place amongst the Alexandrians, when Porphyry limited the range of the metempsychosis, denying that the souls of men ever passed downwards to a lower than the human state. Many of the fathers of the Christian Church espoused it; notably Origen. It was one of the Gnostic doctrines. The Manichæans received it, with much else, from their Zoroastrian predecessors. It was held by Nemesius, who emphatically declares that all the Greeks who believed

in immortality believed also in metempsychosis. There are hints of it in Boethius.
Though condemned, in its Origenistic
form, by the Council of Constantinople in
551, it passed along the stream of Christian theology, and reappeared amongst the
Scholastics in Erigena and Bonaventura.
It was defended with much learning and
acuteness by several of the Cambridge Platonists, especially by Henry More. Glan-
vill devotes a curious treatise to it, the
" Lux Orientalis." English clergy and Irish
bishops were found ready to espouse it.
Many English poets, from Henry Vaughan
to Wordsworth, praise it. It appealed to
Hume, as more rational than the rival theories of Creation and Traduction. It has
points of contact with the anthropology of
Kant and Schelling. It found an earnest
advocate in Lessing. Herder also maintained it, while it fascinated the minds of
Fourier and Lerroux. Soame Jenyns, the
Chevalier Ramsay, and many others have
written in its defense. If we may broadly
classify philosophical systems as *a priori*
or *a posteriori*, intuitional or experiential,
Platonist or Aristotelian, this doctrine will
be found to ally itself, both speculatively

and historically, with the former school of thought.

Passing from the schools to the instinctive ideas of primitive men, or the conceptions now entertained by races half-civilized or wholly barbarous, a belief in transmigration will be found to be almost universal. It is inwoven with nearly all the mythology of the world. It appears in Mexico and in Tibet, amongst the negroes and the Hawaiian Islanders. It comes down from the Druids of ancient Gaul to the Tasmanians of to-day. The stream of opinion, whether instinctive, mystic, or rational, is continuous and broad; and if we could legitimately determine any question of belief by the number of its adherents, the *quod semper, quod ubique, quod ab omnibus*, would apply to this more fitly than to any other. Mr. Tylor speaks of it ("Primitive Culture," ch. xii.) as now "arrested and unprogressive," or lingering only as "an intellectual crotchet." It may be so; but I think it quite as likely to be revived, and to come to the front again, as any rival theory on the subject, when the decay that is the fate of every system of opinion overtakes those that are in the place of honor and recognition now. Each philosophical doctrine being, in the nature of things, only a partial interpretation of the universe, or an approximate solution of the mystery of existence, is in its turn set aside as inadequate; while all the greater ones invariably reappear under altered forms. The resuscitation of discarded theories is as inevitable as the modifications which they undergo in the process of revival. Metempsychosis is true of all *theories*, whether it applies to souls or not.

There are three possible forms of the doctrine. Logically four may be held, but only three are philosophically tenable. Either, first, it may be maintained that the metempsychosis is universal, extending to all finite forms of life, so that the highest may change place with the lowest, and *vice versa*. The life that was in man may degenerate, or pass downwards into the animal; or the life that was in the animal may rise, and pass upwards into man; the winding stream of development flowing either way, and the particular direction which the current takes being determined by the internal state of the individual. There may be thus, on the one hand, deg-

radation and descent ; on the other, elevation and ascent, through a perpetual cycle
of successive births and deaths.   Or, second, the transmigration may be limited to
the animal world, and denied to the human.
It is a conceivable and may seem a plausible hypothesis, to those who shrink from
extending the transmigration to man, that
it applies solely to the lower orders of existence, that the life of an animal is lost
or "blown out," but that on the destruction of its organization, the vital force re-
merges, and is continued in some other
form.   (The supposition which is logically
distinct from this, but which is not philosophically tenable, is the contrary one,
that the transmigration holds good of man
only, and does not extend to the animal
world.)   The third form of the theory is
that the transmigration may apply both to
the human and to the animal world ; but
that in each case it is strictly limited to
one sphere, that is to say, that the souls of
men animate successive bodies, but that
they never descend to a lower level, while
the vital spirit of the animal never ascends
into the human form.   This was practically the development which the Pythago-

rean and Platonic doctrine took, under Porphyry and others, in the Alexandrian school. Thus, metempsychosis may be either, first, a law or process regulating the universal development of life on our planet, or, second, a cyclical movement along one line, and confined to one group of existences; or, third, it may be a movement along two definite lines, but strictly limited to these lines.

There were certain very obvious facts, which gave rise to the belief among primitive races, and others less prominent, though of a higher order, which suggested it to the more meditative spirits of antiquity. The inferences may have been illogically drawn but the natural history of a doctrine is one thing, its philosophical validity is another; and the historical development of a belief does not always or usually follow the lines of scientific evidence. The student of the history of civilization is familiar with this fact, that reasonings which are philosophically worthless have frequently led to conclusions which are at least highly probable; just as beliefs which are demonstratively true have often been sustained by arguments radically unsound.

The superficial resemblances between the lower animals and men, in feature, disposition, and character, in voice and mien, suggested to the primitive races the probability that the bodies of animals were inhabited by human souls, and those of men by animal natures. The intelligence and feeling of the brutes, their half-human character, as well as the brutality of some men, seemed an evidence that their respective souls or vital principles had exchanged places. They saw the cunning of the fox, and the fierceness of the tiger, in their comrades. They also learned the fidelity of a friend from the rare attachment and devotion of their dogs. As they were in the habit of describing the qualities of men by these surface resemblances, as leonine, currish, vulpine, etc., — and, *vice versa*, of describing the characteristics of animals by terms originally applied to their own race, — it was a natural, though not a logical, inference that their respective vital principles were interchangeable. In short, the rare humanity of some animals, and the notorious animality of some men, suggested to the primitive races, not the common origin of both, but the arbitrary passage of one into the other.

In addition, family likenesses being transmitted, and reappearing after an interval of generations, suggested the return of the spirits of the dead within a new physical organization. Mere facial resemblances led the common mind to believe in the reëmbodiment of souls. Still more significantly, the appearance of mental features resembling those of any noted person in the past, suggested the actual return of the departed. If one resembled his ancestors somewhat closely in intellect or valor, in temperament or style of action, it was supposed that the ancestor had again put on the vesture of the flesh, and "revisited the glimpses of the moon." The spirit of the master being seen in the pupil seemed a hint of the same thing; and the notion that one of the dead had returned to reanimate another body very naturally grew out of these obvious concrete facts. It need scarcely be said that the deduction is wholly unwarrantable, and the argument illusory. An illogical inference, founded on some surface analogy, has frequently given rise to a belief, which has grown strong in the total absence of valid evidence in its favor. For example, the spirit of a

master usually appears in his pupil most
conspicuously when both are living, or
shortly after the death of the master, and
when his soul cannot have entered his
pupil, unless he became the recipient of
two souls.   Further, there is no reason to
believe that if metempsychosis took place,
the new manifestations of mind and character would be similar to the old ones.
They would much more likely be widely
different.   It would give us a poor notion
of any spirit that reappeared within the old
limits, if it merely reproduced its past actions.   Such a procedure would be as dis
appointing as those inane utterances of the
dead with which modern Spiritualism pre-
tends to be familiar.   If the spirits of the
departed make any progress in knowledge
and experience, we would expect to find
something very different from a repetition
of their former mode of activity.   The argument is quite illusory.

A third one is much more worthy of con
sideration.   It arises out of certain psychological facts, which have seemed to warrant
the inference of the soul's preëxistence.
Quite suddenly a thought is darted into
the mind, which cannot be traced back to

any source in past experience; or we hear a sound, see an object, experience sensations, which seem to take us wholly out of the circle of sense-perception that has been possible to us in the present life. This is one of the arguments of the Phædo; and it is the central thought of Wordsworth's magnificent "Ode on the Intimations of Immortality from Recollections of Childhood." The "splendor in the grass," and "glory in the flower," which Wordsworth saw and felt in childhood, he explains by their being the dim memory of a brighter experience that was passed; a recovered fragment of ante-natal life —

> Not in entire forgetfulness,
> And not in utter nakedness,
> But trailing clouds of glory do we come, etc.

On the one hand, the halo with which memory surrounds our childhood, and, on the other, the melancholy awakened by a sense of its being irrecoverably gone, have suggested the idea that we look back, as through a golden gateway, to the glory of a dawn preceding it.

> The soul that rises with us, our life's star
> Hath had elsewhere its setting,
> And cometh from afar.

This is also one of the arguments adduced
by Gautama, the reputed founder of the
Nyaya system of Indian Philosophy.   I
quote from the aphorisms of the Nyaya,
published for the Benares College, at Alla-
habad.   "Joy, fear, and grief," he says,
"arise to him that is born, through relation
to his memory of things previously experienced."   And this aphorism is thus com-
mented upon by one of Gautama's pupils,
Viswanatha: "If joy arises before the
causes of joy are experienced, the child
must have existed in a previous life."   And
so the subtile Indian metaphysic said, " If
in one life, then in a series, and an illimitable series ; and there being no beginning,
it is indestructible, and can have no end.
Gautama endeavored to prove the same
thing from the psychological phenomena
of desire.   " We see nothing born void of
desire."   Since every creature experiences
desires which seek satisfaction before there
is any experience of what can satisfy them,
Gautama and his commentator trace this
back to knowledge acquired in a previous
life.

Both arguments are inconclusive.   The
first set of phenomena referred to by Plato,

and by the Platonic poets so often, can be explained otherwise than by the hypothesis of preëxistence. In dreams, notions seemingly the most discordant unite, and our whole consciousness sometimes passes into a chaotic or amorphous state. As to the second set of phenomena appealed to by Gautama, if instinctive desire demands a previous life to explain it, the same instinct in that life requires one still prior, and so on *ad infinitum.* And the action of instinctive desire can be easily explained as the growth of experience, or the result of a series of tentative efforts which seek, and continue to seek, satisfaction, till they find it.

On the other hand, while these suggestions of instinct and of reminiscence seem invalid, the absence of any memory of actions done in a previous state cannot be a conclusive argument against our having lived through it. Forgetfulness of the past may be one of the conditions of entrance upon a new stage of existence. The body, which is the organ of sense-perception, may be quite as much a hindrance as a help to reminiscence. As Plotinus said, "matter is the true river of Lethe:

immersed in it, the soul forgets everything." In that case casual gleams of
memory, giving us sudden, abrupt, and momentary revelations of the past, are precisely the phenomena we would expect to
meet with. If the soul has preëxisted,
what we would *a priori* anticipate are only
some faint traces of recollection, surviving
in the crypts of memory.

One of the main objections brought
against the doctrine of preëxistence — an
objection which seems insuperable to the
popular mind — is the total absence of any
authentic or verifiable memory of the past.
It is supposed that if we cannot remember
a former life, it is all the same as if it never
was ours ; for the thread of identity must
be a conscious one. This, however, is just
what its advocates deny. They appeal to
the latent elements which underlie our
present consciousness, out of which the
clearest knowledge arises ; and they maintain that there is a hidden world of the unconscious in which the subterranean river
of personality flows.

But the deeper and more philosophical
grounds on which the doctrine of the pre-
existence of the soul has been and may be

maintained are threefold. They may be characterized respectively as the speculative, the ethical, and the physical justifications of the dogma. If they explain its prevalence, and account for its vitality, they do so by giving a show of reason for the theory, its intellectual *raison d'être.*

The first is a purely ontological consideration, the relevancy of which will be denied by the disciples of experience, but which seems, to say the least, to be more valid than their denial. No one has stated it with more force or persuasiveness than Plato. The great idealist of antiquity found an evidence of preëxistence in our present knowledge of *a priori* notions, or ideas which are not the product of experience, such as mathematical axioms, and all metaphysical first principles. If they are latent in the soul at birth, their origin must be sought in a previous state of existence. We could not now transcend sense, and reach general notions of any kind, unless these notions had belonged to us in a previous state. But it is evident that if their origin in this life demands for its explanation the presupposition of a prior life, their existence in that state would involve the pos-

tulate of one still previous, and so on *ad
infinitum ;* that is to say, it would demand
the eternal existence of the soul itself.
And it is thus that we reach the fully
developed form of this ontological argument. If life or existence belongs to the
soul intrinsically, it must have always existed. As in the Nyaya system, the soul
is held to be eternal, because, if not eternal,
it would be mortal. " Whatever has had a
beginning will have an end," was the fundamental position of Gautama and his
school ; and this notion is so fixed in the
Brahminical mind, that every religion which
denies it, or fails to recognize it, is looked
upon as *ipso facto* a false religion. The
Brahminical mind is opposed to Christianity, because it conceives that Christianity
is opposed to preëxistence. So in the
Bhagavad Gita it is said of the soul, " You
cannot say it hath been, or is about to be,
or is to be hereafter. It is a thing without birth."

The whole argument of the Phædo re-
volves around the same centre, that the
soul is naturally and intrinsically deathless, that it has in it a principle of life
with which you cannot associate mortal-

ity, and of which you cannot predicate it. If so, its preëxistence is as certain as its posthumous existence. This is the dominant thought of all that Plato teaches on the subject of immortality, alike in the Phædo, the Phædrus, and the Republic. It is a purely ontological consideration. All the detailed argumentation in the Phædo, for example, whether it involves ethical or dialectical elements, — the proof from the everlasting cycle of existence and origination out of opposites, the argument from reminiscence, the proof from the simplicity and consequent indissolubility of the soul, the refutation of the objections of Simmias and Cebes, the psychological plea founded on the native prerogatives and capacities of the soul, — all either presuppose, or are merely different ways of stating and illustrating the cardinal position, that indestructible life belongs to the soul's essence. To Plato, the ideal theory is primary, the immortality of the soul secondary; but the one involves the other. If the mind of man is competent to grasp eternal ideas, it must be itself eternal. If the ideas which it apprehends are eternal, it must participate in their eternity; and this imperish-

ableness is of its very essence. In the
Phædrus the argument is advanced that
the soul is ἀρχὴ κινήσεως. It is the source of
motion ; but having the cause of motion
within itself, out of this αὐτοκίνησις comes its
immortality. In the tenth book of the
Republic the question is raised, what can
possibly destroy the soul ? Evil attacks
and corrupts it. It injures its character
without wasting its substance : and if this,
which most of all might be supposed capable of destroying it, cannot, then nothing
else can assail it. What is composite may
be decomposed ; but the soul, though it
has many faculties, is not composite. It is
one, and cannot be decomposed, and must
therefore live forever. But, if so, it has
lived always. It is without beginning —
ἀεὶ ὄν (Rep. X. 609 – 611) ; as in the
Phædo it is described as ἀίδιον ὄν (106 n.).
The number of souls in the universe does
not increase. An addition to the number
of immortals would be a contradiction in
terms, inasmuch as what begins to be must
die, and what does not die in time was
never born in time. If, therefore, we cannot attach the idea of dissolution or non-
existence to the soul, it must have had an

eternal past; no temporal origin can be assigned to it. Its preëxistence and its posthumous existence are correlative ideas in Platonic thought. If it has had an historical origin in time (which it has), it will have it over and over again; experiencing many births and many deaths. It is born when it dies, and it dies when it is born. In short, the terms "birth" and "death" denote merely relative conceptions; and there disguise our ignorance, as much as they disclose our knowledge. We see the phenomenal appearances of birth and death, of origination and decease; but the amount of vital force, or of spiritual existence, is a fixed and constant quantity.

The second ground on which the theory of preëxistence finds a philosophical justification is an ethical one. It offers an explanation of the moral anomalies of the world, the unequal adjustments of character to situation, with the heterogeneousness and apparent favoritism of Providence. To many minds this has seemed the most plausible aspect under which metempsychosis may be regarded; and if it unravels the ethical puzzle of suffering associated with virtue, and happiness allied with evil, it may have great moral value, even while its scientific basis remains unproved. Hierocles said, "Without the doctrine of metempsychosis, it is not possible to justify the ways of Providence." Let us see. It is offered to us not as an explanation of the origin of evil in the abstract, but as a key to the unequal adjustment of happiness and misery in the present life, or the way in which they are respectively *distributed*. It is an oft-told tale in the literature of the world, and a perplexing fact in every life, this union of virtue with sorrow or even with misery (which is the secret of all tragedy), and the opposite and equally incongruous union of happiness and vice. If the phenomena of the moral world, taken by themselves, are to yield us a theory of the universe, it can scarcely be a monotheistic one. It must be dualistic or Manichean. They seem to indicate either the conspicuous partiality and favoritism of Heaven, or a successful assault on the government of a righteous Being, by a formidable rival power, if not an equal potentate. At this point, the theories of preëxistence and metempsychosis offer to lighten the burden of the difficulty. They affirm, to quote the words of Jouffroy, — used by him in another connection, — that human life is "a drama, whose prologue and catastrophe are both alike wanting." In a previous state, the same laws existed which govern our present life ; and as the two states are connected by moral ties, we now gather the fruit of what we formerly sowed. It is not more true that in age we reap the fruit of the seed we sow in youth, than that we gather in this life the harvest of an innumerable series of past lives. The disasters which overtake the good are not the penalty for present action ; they are punishment for the errors and faults of a bygone life. The sufferers are not expiating their forefathers' crimes, but their own formerly committed. Felicity associated with moral degradation has the same relation to a past state of existence. The reward is given for former actions that were worthy of recompense; the external circumstances of each life having a moral relation to the internal state of the soul in its previous existence.

The theory arises out of a demand for equity in the adjustment of the external and the internal conditions of existence.

On no moral theory can the present unequal adjustment be considered both equitable and final. If it is final — *i. e.*, if there
is no future rectification — it is not equitable. If it is not final, but only a temporary arrangement for the purposes of
moral discipline and education, it may be
the most equitable of all possible arrangements. The moral root of the theory is
thus the sense of justice, and the conviction not only that justice will be done, but
that *it is now being done.* On the theory
of a coming rectification, which connects
the present with the future, and not with
a past life, the idea is that justice is not
now done; but that the assize and the sentence will put all to rights. The theory of
metempsychosis, connecting the present
with the past as well as with the future,
affirms that there is no region of space, or
moment of time, in which it is not done.
It is scarcely to be wondered at that
Henry More, the Cambridge Platonist,
calls this doctrine "the golden key" to
Providence; or that he enlarges in its
praise, in that remarkable dream in his
"Divine Dialogues," in which he describes
his vision of the key. "Let us but as-

sume," he says, "the preëxistence of souls, and all those difficulties which over-cloud the understanding will vanish." He supposes that human souls were created "in infinite myriads," "in the morning of the world." "All intellectual spirits that ever were, are, or shall be, sprang up with the light, and rejoiced together before God, in the morning of the creation." I make this quotation from More — whose Dialogues on the subject are much more interesting than his labored treatise on "The Immortality of the Soul," — because, as he combined the doctrine of the creation of souls with their preëxistence, he represents one branch of the theory; the other branch being that represented by Gautama, Plato, and the neo-Platonists, who maintain the soul's eternity. Metempsychosis fits equally well into both theories. As a speculative doctrine, it is equally consistent with a belief in instantaneous creation, and with a theory of emanation.

The ethical leverage of the doctrine is immense. Its motive power, as compared with the notion of posthumous influence after the individual has perished, — the substitute for immortality offered by La

Mettrie and his colleagues, and by all the positivists, — is great. It reveals as magnificent a background to the present life, with its contradictions and disasters, as the prospect of immortality opens up an illimitable foreground, lengthening out on the horizon of hope. It binds together the past, the present, and the future in one ethical series of causes and effects, the inner thread of which is both personal to the individual and impersonal, connecting him with two eternities, the one behind and the other before. With peculiar emphasis it proclaims the survival of moral individuality and personal identity, along . with the final adjustment of external conditions to the internal state of the agent.

So far the evidence is in favor of the doctrine. Several objections to it from an ethical point of view must now be candidly weighed. To believe in a past state of existence, of which we have no present remembrance, may appear to some minds to weaken the sense of responsibility. It may be doubted whether we can sustain a moral relation to a life of which we remember nothing, or to a future in which the memory of the present will similarly vanish.

To this objection it might justly be replied that the moral links which connect the successive moments of our present experience are often unconscious ones, and their validity as links does not depend on their being luminous ever afterwards. The supposed recency of our origin is not the ground of our responsibility, and we are accountable for a thousand things we have forgotten.

> For is not our first year forgot?
> The haunts of memory echo not,

even as to terrestrial life. To other minds and temperaments, the notion of a vast ancestry, of an illimitable genealogy, will rather deepen the sense of responsibility than weaken it. As the inheritance of an illustrious name and pedigree quickens the sense of duty in every noble nature, a belief in preëxistence may enhance the glory of the present life and intensify the reverence with which the deathless principle is regarded. The want of any definite remembrance of past states of consciousness can be no barrier to a belief in our having experienced them; and a very slight reflection will show that if we have preëxisted this life, memory of the details of the past is absolutely impossible. The power of the conservative faculty, though relatively great, is extremely limited. We forget the larger portion of experience soon after we have passed through it ; and we should be able to recall the particulars of our past years in the present life, filling up the missing links of consciousness since we entered on it, before we were in a position to remember our ante-natal experience. Birth into this world may be necessarily preceded by crossing the river of Lethe, the result being the obliteration of knowledge acquired during a previous state. While the capacity for fresh acquisition survived, the garnered wealth of old experience would determine the amount and the character of the new. So long, therefore, as it is impossible to retain the memory of all past experience in the present life, so long as fragments survive which suggest preëxistence, so long as the river of our consciousness flows in many subterranean ways, so long as the connection of soul and body induces forgetfulness as much as it quickens remembrance, there may be no insuperable barrier in the way of the theory of metempsychosis.

Another difficulty must be considered. It may be said that preexistence fails to explain the moral inequality which now exists, because if we assume a previous life to account for the maladjustment of this, a prior preëxistence must explain the anomalies of that, and so on *ad infinitum.* Even if the moral disorder is temporary, its future elimination will not explain why it once existed under a perfect system of moral government. The theory of its previous existence only carries the difficulty one stage nearer to its source, but it does not remove it, or lighten its pressure in the region to which it is driven back. Besides, if the ultimate prospect is such a re-arrangement of destiny, by an adjustment of the external state to the internal condition, that no inequality remains, why is this not effected *now?* Why is the marriage of virtue and felicity (the internal and the external) so long postponed?

To this it may be replied that it is no part of the theory of metempsychosis to explain the origin of evil. It is only the inequality arising from the way in which happiness and misery are distributed in this life — often in inverse ratio to virtue and vice — that it seeks to explain. To throw any speculative or moral difficulty into the background, and prevent its forward pressure, is to accomplish something, although the puzzle still remains ; and to throw it back a little way is perhaps all that we can do, unless we can eliminate it, which assuredly we cannot do. The demand to carry it still farther back, so as to explain the previous inequality, is really to raise the question why it is there at all. And to this there is probably no answer, except that which the existence of free will supplies. With free will permanently existing, there is a permanent possibility of departure from the moral centre, and of swerving towards the circumference. Hence the necessity for a readjustment of internal with external conditions will always exist.

Others may still further object that their sense of justice is not satisfied by our suffering in the present life for the errors of one that is past. But is there justice in our suffering in manhood for the faults of our youth? in our receiving anything to-day for the acts of yesterday? or in children suffering at all for the deeds of their parents? In the two former cases, it is merely a question of a certain time elapsing between the act and its consequences. The third is the case of one individual suffering for the errors of another, to whom he stands organically and otherwise related. But if each of us may suffer for his own past actions, and one may suffer through another's deeds, the law will continue to operate, although the deed may belong to one stage of being and the penalty to another, although the cause and its consequence be separated by the widest possible interval.

There is a third objection which must not be overlooked. An everlasting cycle of lives might become wearisome, and induce a longing for repose, unbroken by any new birth in time. The perpetual descent and ascent, with repetitions of experience only slightly varied, might lead to the wish of the lotus-eaters —

> While all things else have rest from weariness,
> All things have rest, why should we toil alone?
> .   .   .   .
> Nor ever fold our wings,
> And cease our wanderings;
> Why should we only toil, the roof and crown of things?

This is virtually the longing for *nirvana*.

And the relation of the doctrine of metempsychosis to that of nirvana is curious
and interesting. Metempsychosis is part
of the Buddhist belief, and yet nirvana,
the goal of Buddhist longing, is the cessation of metempsychosis; the soul attaining rest by ceasing to exist, or being
"blown out."   Into all the forms of Buddhist opinion transmigration enters; but
"soul wandering" is a calamity, an evil
inseparable from existence. Nirvana is a
deliverance from metempsychosis. After
undergoing the needful purification of
many births and deaths, the soul attains
the condition requisite for the perfect felicity of annihilation. In other words, it is
the discipline of metempsychosis that
gradually induces a feeling of detachment
from sensible things. A repetition of experience is no longer necessary, and the
soul is at length fitted and entitled to escape from the turmoil of existence, with its
endless "vanity and vexation of spirit,"
into the perfect rest of non-existence.
Such is nirvana. It is worthy of note,
however, that amongst the Cingalese
Buddhists, the transmigration ending in
nirvana — or the peace of nonentity —

passed into a doctrine of extinction plus transmission. The departing soul, ready to be "blown out," lit the lamp of existence in another spirit before its own annihilation was consummated. Its last point of contact with existence, its expiring effort, was a creative one. It kept up the succession of creatures destined to undergo the same process of metempsychosis, by a final act of *upadana*, or attachment to existence ; after which, it entered itself into the supreme bliss of nirvana.

This desire for rest in the extinction of all desire, so congenial to the Oriental mind, presents no attraction to the hardier races of the West and North. It may be, in fact, a temperamental feature, determined by subtle climatic conditions and racial peculiarities. Certainly it offers no allurement to natures that have learned to measure the charm of existence by the amount of energy evoked and sustained ; and who have seen that "pleasure is but the reflex of unimpeded energy." Rest is only valued by us as the condition of a fresh departure, and of renewed activity. Tarrying for a time in any harbor of existence, the inevitable longing arises for another sight of the great ocean, and a new voyage.

The last ground on which metempsychosis may be advocated belongs to the metaphysic of physics. As an argument it has often been implied, when it has not been expressly affirmed ; just as the imaginative guesses and surmisings of the primitive tribes may have grown unconsciously out of a speculative root, which their authors were incompetent to grasp. That philosophical root is the uniformity in the amount of spiritual existence ; the conviction that, since the quantity of matter is neither increased nor diminished, it is the same with the quantity of spirit ; that it is neither added to, nor taken from, at any moment of time. It is a doctrine of modern science that there is a uniform stock of energy within the universe, which neither increases nor decreases, but which incessantly changes its form and manifestations, dissolving retiring reëmerging, appearing disappearing and returning, — the proteus of the physical world. Is there a phœnix in the spiritual realm, corresponding to this proteus in the material sphere? In other words, while the amount of material substance remains stationary, if the quantity of spiritual existence were swiftly to increase at one end, with no corresponding diminution at the other, *i. e.*, if the birth of the spirits of the human race was a new creation, — multitudes every instant of time darting out of nonentity into manifested being, — and if their death was a simple transference to some new abode, would not this incessant and rapid increase overstock the universe?

Now, since no physical power is ever lost, all force being simply transformed, if the doctrine of the conservation of energy be applied to the sphere of moral and spiritual life, two alternative theories alone are possible: either preëxistence and immortality combined, or emanation and absorption. Whether the latter is materialistic or pantheistic matters not, except for the name we choose to adopt; the essence of the doctrine is the same. It is self-evident that if the amount of spiritual existence is *not* increased every moment, the preëxistence of all souls that are born, before their incarnation in the flesh, is as certain as their immortality. The one carries the other with it, or is carried by it. They are, indeed, not two doctrines, but two sides of the same doctrine. Thus the number of souls in the universe will be a fixed and constant quantity. If the conservation of energy be true of spiritual existence, and the soul is to survive the death of the body, then it lived before the body was vitalized. If it is never to be extinguished, it never was produced. It was probably the force of this consideration that led the acute mind of David Hume to affirm that " metempsychosis is the only system of this kind (*i. e.*, of immortality) that Philosophy can hearken to."[1] He "says what is incorruptible must also be ingenerable." "The soul, if immortal, existed before our birth" (p. 400). In the same connection he acutely suggests "how to *dispose of* the infinite number of posthumous existences ought to embarrass the religious theory" (p. 404). With this we may associate a remark of Shelley: "If there are no reasons to suppose that we have existed before that period at which our existence apparently commences, then there are no grounds for supposing that we shall continue to exist after our exist-

---

[1] *Philosophical Works*, iv. p. 404.

ence has apparently ceased." (Essays, p. 58). The "continual influx of beings," without a corresponding egress, is a difficulty which will seem insuperable to many minds. There is a growing *consensus* of opinion amongst spiritualists and materialists alike, that the quantity both of matter and of force within the universe suffers no diminution, and no enlargement; loss in one direction being invariably and necessarily balanced by gain in another, and all the phenomenal changes in Nature being simply a matter of exchange — a transposition of elements, the sum of which is constant. If this be so, it has an important bearing both on the survival of the soul after death, and on its preëxistence; the two doctrines standing and falling together.

As to the permanence of the materials which compose the body, when the organization is broken up and disintegrated, there is no debate. The survival, in some form or other, of what we call the mind, soul, or conscious ego, and what a materialist psychology terms vital force, is also conceded. Neither is annihilated; they are only transmuted or transformed. But the controversy remains after this concession, and underlies it. The alterations which the body undergoes can be traced, because it continues visible after death. Its changes can be experimentally investigated, because the transformations are slowly effected. But the transformations and changes of the soul, or vital principle, cannot be traced.

The question which now remains to be disposed of, on grounds of probability, is not whether the soul does or does not survive. Its survival is conceded, and maintained as axiomatic. The only controversy is, *in what form does it survive?* Is it refunded to the universe, as material substance is restored, to be worked up into new forms, by the protoplastic force that originally made it what it was? or does it survive, with its individuality and identity unbroken? *That* is the controversy between the materialist and the spiritualist.

May not the latter be abandoning one half of his territory, or at least surrendering one of his positions and weakening his ultimate defense, if he throws away the doctrine of preëxistence? It seems difficult to maintain, on rational grounds, that the sum of finite existence is being perpetually filled up before, with no corresponding diminution behind ; a distinctly quantitative increase in front, with no decrease to balance it in the rear. Over-population in the mother country has necessitated emigration to the colonies. But, on the theory of incessant miraculous increase, there is no conceivable colony in the universe that would not be already overstocked, and where the arrival of any emigrants from the parent country would not be unwelcome.

In this connection, it is worthy of note with what caprice the immortality of the brute creation is sometimes spoken of, in comparison with the immortality of man. By many, who are confident of their own survival, the immortality of animals is considered a curious and interesting question, but one that is speculatively unimportant, and theoretically indeterminable. How much depends on the solution of the problem of the destination of *life* is not perceived. For example, we hear it often said, there can be no objection to the immortality of the *higher* animals. But scientific rigor will not permit a line of demarkation to be drawn between the animal races. They all shade into one another. Are we then prepared to admit the immortality of every creature in which there is the faintest adumbration of intelligence? and if so, of every one in which is "the breath of life." If we do not admit this, then the intelligence which we find in the dog, the beaver, the bee, and the ant, which does not "perish everlastingly," is *conserved* somewhere, after the dissolution of the bodies of these animals. But how vast the Hades, stocked with the spiritual part of every creature that has ever lived and died upon our planet from primeval time! When the prolific increase of the tribes of animated nature is realized, and the enormous cycles of time during which the succession has been kept up, imagination sinks paralyzed before the conception of any shadowy storehouse, in which these creatures continue to live, far less to flourish. The supposition is *felo-de-se*.

But, it may be pertinently asked, if we abandon the immortality of all, can we retain the immortality of any? Is not transmigration, in this case, the most probable hypothesis? Is not the notion of a uniform stock of vital energy, which passes and repasses endlessly throughout the organized tribes of nature, the most consistent theory we can frame? No one need hesitate to apply the doctrine of metempsychosis to the animal world, although he may doubt its applicability to the human race; while, if we reject it in the lower sphere, and, in consequence, hold that the intelligence and devotion of the dog perish, it may be hard to maintain that the reason and affection of man survive.

Another special difficulty arises at this point, and it is, perhaps, the chief objection to the doctrine of metempyschosis. How does "the life" that survives unextinguished pass from one organized form to another? We can trace its signs or manifestations till they cease at death. So far all is clear. But what *becomes* of it on the dissolution of the body?

> Animula, vagula, blandula,
> Hospes comesque corporis,
> *Quæ nunc abibis in loca?*

If not extinguished, it merely retreats and reappears. But how does it connect itself with the new organization, into which it subsequently enters as an animating and vitalizing principle? This is a difficulty not only in the way of transmigration, but of survival in any form. The present connection between soul and body is known so far ; and, in the absence of experience of separation, we have some psychological facts which suggest that the union is not inseparable, that the soul is not a function of the body, but that in each individual we have two principles, if not two substances, temporarily united. When they are separated, however, as they are at death, how does the spiritual part continue to live disembodied? and how does it unite itself, or how is it united, with a new corporeal form? Does it ally itself with its new organization, in some cases, by a voluntary act? in others, by a passive and involuntary process? If the latter, there must be some law by which the change is effected, some method of development determining the movement in a cycle. If the act is voluntary, we have a fresh difficulty to face, viz., that the spiritual must be able to select its new abode. It must, therefore, either choose one out of many, or it must enter into the only one that is fitted for its reception. It must be either wholly active or wholly passive, or partly active and partly passive.

We can state the alternatives, but how to choose amongst them, how to select one of them, is a difficulty that remains. The spirit shrinks from a ghostly or disembodied state as its perpetual destiny, nearly as much as it recoils from the sleep of nirvana; but how to find a body, how to incarnate itself, or even to conceive the process by which it could by any foreign agency be robed anew, remains a puzzle; even while, as Henry Vaughan expresses it, —

> It feels through all this fleshly dresse
> Bright shootes of everlastingnesse.

These are difficulties which attend every attempt to form definite conceptions as to the details of this question. Mr. Greg is wise when he says, of the belief in immortality, "Let it rest in the vague, if you would have it rest unshaken,"

An additional point must be noted. Although we may validly object to have our convictions exhibited to view, as we decline to expose the rootlets of a plant to "the nipping and the eager air" of winter, it is a signal gain to integrity of belief that the scientific spirit of our age demands the removal of all presuppositions which cannot be verified, and insists that those which remain shall be luminous from root to branch. It does this with even more force and rigor than Descartes employed, in his new method of research. So much intellectual mist has been allowed to gather and settle over this question of the soul's destiny, that when a breath of the east wind raises it, and shows how little is known or can be intelligently surmised, many desire that the obscuring curtain should speedily fall again. But in discussing the question of immortality it is above all things necessary that we mark the *alternatives* of the controversy, and the consequences which follow from our premises, alike of affirmation and denial. If we reject the doctrine of preëxistence we must either believe in non-existence, or fall back on one or other of the two opposing theories of creation and traduction: and, as we reject extinction, we may find that preëxistence has fewer dificulties to face than the rival hypotheses. Creation — or creationism, as it has sometimes been named — is the theory that every moment of time multitudes of new souls are simultaneously born, not sent down from a celestial source, but freshly made out of nothing, and placed in bodies prepared for them by a process of natural generation. It is curious to observe how vehemently the Cambridge Platonists recoiled from the notion of a pure spirit, fresh from the hand of Deity, being placed by him "in such a body as would presently defile his image." The idea of the Creator being *compelled* to add a spirit to the body, however and whensoever a body might arise, according to natural law and process, seemed to them a monstrous infraction of divine liberty. The theory of traduction seemed to them even worse, as it implied the derivation of the soul from at least two sources — from both parents; and a substance thus derived was apparently composite and quasi-material.

It is easy to criticise the doctrine of preëxistence, as held in the Pythagorean brotherhood, and taught by the mystic sage of Agrigentum, or even by Plato. The fantastic folly of the Brahminical teaching (as in the twelfth book of the laws of Manu) and the absurdity of Buddha's transmigrations are apparent. But it is easier to follow Lucretius in his satire

of it, than to appreciate the difficulty which
gave it birth. As reproduced by Virgil
and by Cicero, the genius of the Greek
poets and philosophers lost the charm of
its original setting; and I question if the
surmises of Plato were fully appraised, till
the Phædo itself experienced metempsychosis in Wordsworth's "Ode." But
stripped of all extravagance, and expressed
in the modest terms of probability, the
theory has immense speculative interest,
and great ethical value. It is much to
have the puzzle of the origin of evil
thrown back for an indefinite number of
cycles of lives, to have a workable explanation of *nemesis*, and of what we are accustomed to call the moral tragedies, and the
untoward birth of a multitude of men and
women. It is much, also, to have the doctrine of immortality lightened of its difficulties; to have our immediate outlook
relieved by the doctrine that, in the soul's
eternity, its preëxistence and its future
existence are one. The retrospect may
assuredly help the prospect. And if "this
gray dogma, fairly clear of doubt," as Glan-
vill describes it, seems strange in the absence of all remembered traces of past

existence, it is worth considering that in a future state a point will be reached when preëxistence will be true. If we are to be immortal, immediately after death metempsychosis will have become a realized experience; and our present lives will stand in the same relation to the future, on which we shall then have entered, as that in which the past now stands to our present life.

Henry More said that he produced his golden key of preëxistence "only at a dead lift, when no other method would satisfy him, touching the ways of God, that by this hypothesis he might keep his heart from sinking." Whether we make use of it or not, we ought to realize its alternatives. They are these. Either all life is extinguished and resolved, through an absorption and reassimilation of the vital principle everywhere; or a perpetual miracle goes on, in the incessant and rapid increase in the amount of spiritual existence within the universe; and while human life survives, the intelligence and the affection of the lower animals perish everlastingly.